ALSO BY ZOSIA MAMET

My First Popsicle

DOES THIS
MAKE ME FUNNY?

Essays

—≪≪◆≫≫—

ZOSIA MAMET

VIKING

VIKING
An imprint of Penguin Random House LLC
1745 Broadway, New York, NY 10019
penguinrandomhouse.com

An earlier version of "Mirror Mirror" first appeared as "How a Month Without Mirrors Set Me Free" on *Refinery29* in 2019. An earlier version of "It's in Your Head" was read at the AOL Makers Forum, 2017.

Designed by Cassandra Garruzzo Mueller

LIBRARY OF CONGRESS CATALOGING-IN-PUBLICATION DATA
Names: Mamet, Zosia, 1988– author.
Title: Does this make me funny? : essays / Zosia Mamet.
Description: New York : Viking, 2025.
Identifiers: LCCN 2024056958 (print) | LCCN 2024056959 (ebook) |
ISBN 9780593490563 (hardcover) | ISBN 9780593490570 (ebook)
Subjects: LCSH: Mamet, Zosia, 1988– | Television actors and actresses—United
States—Biography. | Essays. lcgft | Autobiographies. lcgft
Classification: LCC PN1992.4.M275 A3 2025 (print) |
LCC PN1992.4.M275 (ebook) | DDC 791.4502/8092 [B]—dc23
LC record available at https://lccn.loc.gov/2024056958
LC ebook record available at https://lccn.loc.gov/2024056959

Printed in the United States of America
1st Printing

The authorized representative in the EU for product safety and compliance is Penguin Random House Ireland, Morrison Chambers, 32 Nassau Street, Dublin D02 YH68, Ireland, https://eu-contact.penguin.ie.

*To all the good souls who have made
my life better for their presence in it.
You know who you are. This is for you xx.*

"I fear I am a relic, and I have misplaced my tambourine."

MOTHER SUPERIOR, *SISTER ACT*

Contents

Part 3: Astronomical Twilight

Introduction

GHOST LIGHT

My mother likes to say that I was born onstage.

She was pregnant with me during a production of *The Cherry Orchard*. So technically that was my first job. There are photographs of her sitting in a rocking chair, long curly strawberry-blond wig falling around her shoulders and my tiny form kicking somewhere inside her stomach. Growing up, I loved that idea—that my cells were forming themselves onstage in front of an audience while my mother said some of the finest theatrical words ever written. That theater was infused into my bones, that I was born to be an actress. I loved the romance of this notion. And the thought that if I was incubated under the ghost light perhaps I wasn't just *born* but *destined* to be an actress. This fantasy has brought me solace during many dark nights of the soul. Because you can't be denied your destiny, right? Don't worry, I am very aware of how delusional this sounds.

My mother is not the only family member whose artistic leanings contributed to who I am today.

John, my great-grandfather on my mother's side, was an author and a titan of academia. He was also, apparently, a philandering asshole. The latter part was conveniently left out of the history books given the rest of his impressive résumé. He was the first president of the Juilliard School, and while teaching at Columbia he started the Great Books program, a curriculum that identifies key books in Western literature. (In high school, I dropped out of the program a week in after I found out we'd have to read and annotate *Swann's Way* over a single weekend. No thank you.) My great-grandfather published numerous books in his lifetime, which was maybe the reason he didn't have any spare time to father the children he'd created within his one legal marriage, let alone any children that may have existed from his extracurricular activities. My family doesn't talk about him much.

Russell, my maternal grandfather, was a famous playwright. He was twenty years my grandmother's senior and died when my mother was only sixteen, so I'm not exactly sure what he was like as a father, husband, or grandfather. But like my great-grandfather, he left a mark with his career. He wrote the book for *The Sound of Music*, among other plays, with his partner Howard Lindsay, my mother's namesake.

My maternal grandmother, Anna, was his dutiful sidekick, playing perfectly the part of "wife of" to the arts and literary elite of New York during the golden age of theater. But she also made a name for herself in her own right by helping to revitalize Lincoln Center and most importantly, in my opinion, creating TKTS: a ticket booth in Times Square that sells half-priced theater tickets, making theater more affordable and accessible to the masses. She believed theater was important—something that should be enjoyed by everyone.

Due to her parents' storied background, my mother grew up among the New York theater and literary elite. Eugene O'Neill was her godfather. I once found a letter from him to my grandparents while I was snooping through my grandmother's basement. He was congratulating them on my mother's birth. Within the same box were personal letters from Robert Frost to my grandmother and a copy of *Vogue* that my mother and uncle were featured in as children.

My father was born in Chicago. His father was a union lawyer for the Teamsters. Both of my paternal grandparents died before I was born. I don't know much of them other than what I've been told. There are differing stories from both of my parents, but the overall sentiment is that both my paternal grandfather and grandmother were harsh people, judgmental people, at times violent people with whom my father did not get along very well. And so he struck out on his own at quite a young age in order to make a name for himself and forge his own path.

He likes to tell a story that he marched into the office of the most high-powered theater producer in Chicago with a copy of his first Broadway play, *American Buffalo*. And without a penny to his name, he threw the play down onto the producer's desk (they had hard copies in those days—I know, what a novelty) and said, "If that play doesn't win the Pulitzer Prize I'll pay you five thousand dollars." It didn't, but his next one did.

My parents supposedly met after my father saw my mother in a movie. He rushed over to his friend's dressing room at whatever Broadway house he was working at and said, "I just saw the woman I'm going to marry in a film. Her name is Lindsay Crouse." And his friend said, "Well, if you want to get in touch with her, she's at my apartment right now because we're dating." The details are fuzzy from there, but they fell in love hard and fast and were married six months later.

Relationships are hard. Marriage is hard. Marriage in the entertainment industry is hard. Marriage in the entertainment industry between two—what's a nice word for "difficult"? If you can think of it please insert that here—artists is hard. I love my parents but I cannot imagine being married to either one of them, so it's no surprise to me that they had a hard time being married to each other. I came later on in their marriage and their divorce was finalized before my first birthday. I have no recollection of them together, which to me is a blessing. There's nothing to compare it to; there is no nuclear family unit that I am missing, because I never had one.

We all lived in Cambridge, Massachusetts, for a while. Until my mother moved my sister and me out to Los Angeles when I was five and time with my father was relegated to his sporadic visits at the Bel-Air or the Beverly Hills Hotel. We'd spend hours in the pool and order room service and eat Toblerone from the minibar. I loved my father but I saw him rarely. Again, stories differ here as to why our visits were so infrequent, but in my opinion the truth always lies somewhere in the middle.

My father met my stepmother while she was doing a play of his on the West End. She was a young actress and musician who he swept off her feet. The recurrent theme here is that he's good at that. They were married by the time I was three and my two half-siblings came soon after that.

My mother remarried when I was eleven to a man she had met when I was eight. He came with a son from a previous marriage, two years my junior. I put my stepfather through the wringer to start but came to love him deeply over the years. He was a TV editor and director, so it seems as if there is no escaping the industry from any side of what my high school boyfriend liked to refer to as my family woodpile.

By now, you get the idea: I am the product of well-known, successful arts and entertainment humans. And, even though in my self-deprecating artistic brain I don't yet have the career I want and I spend an unhealthy amount of time thinking about women my age who do and wishing them not harm, per se, but maybe hoping that they'd change their names and move to Siberia for a few years and give me a shot at bat for a while, to most people I have had a very successful career, for which I am eternally grateful.

One could also say this lineage makes me a nepo baby. That being said, there are many successful actresses out there far more beautiful and interesting with WAAAAAY more famous legacies than mine. So if I'm a nepo baby I'm like a B minus one at best and maybe not even a full one. I'm like a nepo baby lite, a nepito baby, if you will.

The one advantage being born into the industry gave me was knowledge. I went into acting without any questions about what this life was going to entail. I was exposed to it from the moment I came online as a human, so I didn't have any illusions about the path I was choosing. But when I first started out, I also found people were much harder on me because they explicitly didn't want to give me a leg up given my heritage, AND they expected to be blown away every time I walked into a room. I mean, obviously I want to blow your socks off anytime I open my mouth in an audition, but also, when you're reading for Cheerleader #3 in a Disney movie of the week and you have four lines, one of which is something along the lines of "Jason's party is gonna rock," it's a little hard to show your Oscar-worthy range.

So yes, technically, am I a product of my lineage and upbringing? Yes. Does that make me a nepo baby? Technically, probably, yes. Did I also work my motherfucking ass off, crawling on my hands and knees up the nonexistent ladder of the entertainment industry, trudging against high winds and a backwards tide and people telling me for the better part of a decade not to quit my day job?

Abso-fucking-lutely.

And while I come from a family of artists, I have also often wondered if I was left on the doorstep, the unwanted offspring of the milkman. I say this because I have never entirely felt like I fit in with them.

I have always also felt like a misfit within my family, my peers, my industry, this world. A square peg in a round hole. I don't think this is unique to me and I don't say this to garner your sympathy, but just so you know where I'm coming from. Even as I write this I think, Where will this book fit? Why am I publishing it? Perhaps it will make for a nice coaster on people's coffee tables or a prop for an uneven chair. The generational buildup of many decades of artistic self-deprecation is strong within me.

I will stop stalling now and let you read what is essentially my diary. I'm not gonna lie, I feel pretty arrogant publishing this and thinking anyone will enjoy it, but the desire to make people laugh or cry or just MAYBE applaud me for something I have done and fill the void within me far outweighs the fear. So without further ado, here are some stories about my life so far. Whether or not you like them, I do hope just maybe they help you feel less alone.

XX

ZM

Part 1

-≪≪◆≫≫-

The Headache Park

SANTA? BABY?

When I was little I believed in magic. Fairies, wizards, talking animals, portals to other worlds through mundane cupboards— I wholeheartedly embraced all of it.

I would build tiny houses in our backyard and hide in the bushes waiting for fairies to come reside within them. I was convinced that once the fairies met me we would become fast friends. I watched *Escape to Witch Mountain* on repeat trying to study how I could unlock the purple magic within myself. Whenever I met an older woman I would stare deep into her eyes searching for any hint of purple in them trying to deduce if perhaps she was a witch. I set traps for the Easter Bunny, hoping that if I caught him maybe he would bring me back to his magical corner of the world. I read and reread the Narnia books hunting for a clue about where in MY closet I could find the portal that would lead me to my freedom. I also read *A Wrinkle in Time, Alice's Adventures in Wonderland, The Phantom Tollbooth*, and the like, each of these books igniting a desperation within me to find the magical realms they described.

I was consumed by the need to find my way out of my daily run-of-the-mill reality and into one of the better, magical worlds I loved so deeply. And so I created rules to follow that I thought would help me get there.

If I didn't cross my fingers when I said out loud something I wished for, I wouldn't get it. If I didn't knock on wood when I talked about something I was scared of, something worse would happen. If I slept facing the window, then the monsters wouldn't come for me. If I circled the tree ten times repeating "I believe, I believe, I believe" and left a trail of cherry seeds back to my house, then fairies would show up. If I didn't jump five feet away from my bed when I went to pee in the middle of the night, then the monster living underneath my bed would most definitely grab me by the ankles, slice my Achilles tendons with its talons, and drag me to hell on its back.

I was, self-admittedly, a child with a wild imagination. I would talk to myself a ton, create entire worlds inside my mind with just myself and a couple of sticks in the backyard. I'd play mermaid in our pool. I stretched the boundaries of thought in a fanciful way on a daily basis.

All the therapists I've ever had call this magical thinking mixed with OCD. But I think it was simply survival. If I focused on the magical rules I believed I had to follow, on rituals, on books and stories and believing in worlds beyond the one I knew, then I didn't have to think as much about the fact that my lunch was going to be stolen that day, just like every other day. I didn't have to think about the fact that I didn't have friends. I didn't have to feel the deep, overwhelming sadness of being unliked.

Finding the portal to Narnia wasn't a short-term goal; I knew it was going to take time and research and patience. So while I hunted for my big ticket out, I also found smaller ways to help me escape while stuck within the confines of my reality.

Nature was a big one for me. I would hide in the hills behind my house and find places where I couldn't see the homes below. I would pretend that I was the only person left in the world and that it was just me and the animals from then on. I would make plans for where I would sleep and how I would get water and what I would eat.

The barn was another place of escape for me. Horses saved my life growing up. They were honestly my only true friends. When I was with them, I could finally feel at ease. They made me feel whole and worthy. Riding grounded me, but it also gave me hope that there was something bigger than my mundane existence out there and I just had to keep searching for it.

But my biggest escape was Christmas.

Christmas was the physical and emotional jackpot of my childhood Indiana Jones hunt for magic and freedom.

I grew up in Los Angeles, but every year, we'd migrate back east to my grandmother's for Christmas break. To me, it was the most magical time of year. Not only because Hallmark had programmed me to think so but because it was two-plus weeks where I got to completely forget about the hell that was my school life and immerse myself within the all-encompassing magic of Christmas.

My grandmother created the most gorgeous rituals. We'd decorate the tree together, which would take hours because every ornament had a specific history that she would regale me with. We'd bake together, watch all the Christmas classics; we'd wrap presents, carol on Christmas Eve, gorge ourselves on clementines that she'd buy by the boxful. I loved every second of it.

My biggest Christmas turn-on was Santa Claus.

Get your mind out of the gutter! I was a child—I didn't want to fuck him. But that man? That man represented the most important thing in the world to me: escape. Because if he was real it meant that there was a world outside of the one that I currently resided so miserably inside of. And his world was beautiful and filled with magic and kindness and snow and you could eat as much sugar as you wanted and never get diabetes. If Santa Claus was real, then maybe one day I could leave this godforsaken place behind and go be a hot cocoa barista at the North Pole and finally be happy. I clung to the idea of him with the grip of someone hanging off the side of a very tall building. I NEEDED him to be real.

And then, one year, when I was seven, the unimaginable happened.

It was a Christmas Eve like any other. We had dinner, we went caroling, we came home and opened one present each. We made a plate of treats for Santa and one for his reindeer and left them out by the fireplace along with his yearly thank-you note for being Santa Claus. We got ready for bed and snuggled in for the night. I had a ritual of sleeping underneath my bed on Christmas Eve. For some reason I loved it. It made the night somehow seem more magical, more special, singular. The magic of Christmas even erased my pathological fear of the monsters that I normally believed lived under the bed. Even they couldn't touch me on Christmas.

I'd obviously seen every Christmas movie under the sun and dreamt of living out one of those scenes where the little girl wakes up to Santa putting presents underneath the tree and he shushes her and says, Go back to sleep, little one, you've been a good girl. (In retrospect, this sounds slightly creepy, but you get what I mean.) I wanted to meet the man. I wanted to know without a shadow of a doubt that he was real. And that night, for a split second, I thought my dreams were going to come true.

I woke with a start having heard a thud. I immediately thought, Whoa, this is my lucky day, that's the sound of reindeer landing on the roof. And then I heard voices in the living room. That's when I really started to freak.

I was going to meet Santa Claus.

I tried to level my breathing so as not to seem too scattered. I wanted to be calm, cool, and collected, and to have a proper conversation with the guy. So I crawled out from under the bed, smoothed out my pajamas, and walked out of the bedroom and into the living room. What I saw was a catastrophe.

My mother was in the living room PUTTING FUCKING PRESENTS UNDER THE MOTHERFUCKING TREE. It's funny how bad our bullshit meter is as kids. Children naturally see the best in people and give them the benefit of the doubt. Which makes us believe adults when they lie to us. Especially our parents. But I could see it in my mother's eyes when she saw me standing there slack-jawed and terrified. She knew she was caught. She covered well, but deep down in my heart I knew. I fucking knew.

"Honey! What are you doing up?" she asked, her voice five octaves higher than usual.

I told her I thought I'd heard something. That I thought I'd heard Santa.

She told me she thought she'd forgotten a couple of Santa's snacks so she'd come out just to double-check everything was in order. "You know how far he has to travel tonight; we want to make sure he has enough sugar to help keep him awake!"

She shooed me back to bed and tucked me back in.

I let her. I was too shocked and afraid of what I thought I knew to delve any deeper that night. So I let the usual magic of Christmas Eve and the stalworthy belief I'd had up until about twenty minutes before lull me to sleep.

The next morning, we went through all the magnificent motions. I allowed myself to enjoy it, but I was only half there—as if I were an observer, like Scrooge being taken around by the ghosts.

After all of the presents had been opened and the wrapping paper had been crumpled into trash bags and pancakes had been eaten, I grabbed my mother's hand and led her to the couch. I sat her down and looked her straight in the eye and asked her not to lie to me. I asked her to promise to tell me the truth, that I could handle it and I wanted to know, that I needed to know. And I asked her if Santa was real.

And she stared back at me and she told me that he was. She swore on everything I loved that he was. She told me that I had to keep believing and she promised she would never lie to me. And I trusted her.

Because I had her word to hang it on, I doubled down on my belief. And I hung on for far too long. When kids at school would make fun of me or tell me I was crazy or that their parents had told them the truth, I would scoff and feel sorry for them because they just didn't know how to believe. I had seen my mother, I had caught her red-handed, I had given her a perfect opportunity to lay it all out for me, but she had reassured me. Obviously they were wrong.

Given how tightly held my belief was, it's funny that I actually don't remember the exact moment I stopped believing. If I'm being honest with myself I think it must have been that night when I was seven. My heart knew but I wasn't ready then to let go. Eventually I did, though, mostly because the teasing had gotten so bad. And life went on, a little less magically, but I survived.

Years later, as a young adult, I was living in New York and spending my first Christmas by myself. I was on the outs with certain members of my family at the time and the ones I was on the ins with were traveling for the holiday. I was semi-new to New York and I didn't have a ton of friends, and the ones I did have had either flown home to their own families or gone on vacation. I was starting rehearsals for my first play on January 2 and I was terrified. I was the lead and the only TV actress in the cast and I was desperate to make a good impression. So I'd opted to stay in the city by myself and work on my lines, preparing for my first day of rehearsal. I thought it would be nice and productive and quiet.

I wasn't prepared for the absolutely bone-crushing amount of loneliness I felt being young and single and effectively friendless in New York City during Christmas. The isolation knocked the wind out of me. On Christmas morning, I took a walk to try to shake off the sadness. I thought if someone saw me walking down the street with a coffee and dressed in outside clothes—hard pants with a zipper, a bra, etc.—as opposed to the pajamas I'd been in for the last I don't know how many days, they'd think, Oh hey, there's a person who's just doing life. She looks normal and content and not like she's slowly melting under the acid rain of sorrow and friendlessness that follows her everywhere.

So I got myself out, ordered my coffee, and started walking the fiftyish blocks uptown to stare at the Rockefeller tree. A dose of Christmas magic to salve my weeping heart. It was freezing that year, and I was bundled up to my eyeballs in layers trying to keep out the bone-chilling wind.

It was when I rounded the corner from my street onto Houston that I saw him, in all his red velvet glory. He was running down the middle of the street, his long white beard flapping in the wind. Suddenly, I was seven again, standing in pajamas, staring at the Christmas tree. I couldn't move. I had to stop myself from whispering, "Santa, is that you?"

But then he multiplied, and where there had been one, there was now a hundred, and all of a sudden, I was surrounded by Santa Clauses rushing past me at full tilt. Some were gorgeous, some were trashy, some were barely dressed. Classic Santa, drag Santa, slutty Santa, pretty much every version was wildly drunken Santa.

I couldn't move, I just stood there as they rushed past. It was like I'd been transported inside a snow globe and instead of snowflakes, Santa Clauses of all shapes and sizes were falling down around me.

Traffic had come to a standstill. As I took in the spectacle, a woman got out of her cab in a furious huff, yelling back at the cabbie, "I'll fucking walk from here." As she passed, pulling on her gloves and hitching her coat tighter, she shook her head and said, "I fucking hate SantaCon."

And I get it. To most, SantaCon, the annual pub crawl where people from all over the city dress as Santa, is just an excuse for frat guys and overworked hedge fund managers to hide behind the beloved disguise of the red suit and roam the streets of New York wreaking infuriating and annoying drunken havoc, crowding the subways, stopping traffic, and pissing in the middle of the street.

But every year when SantaCon rolls around, there's always still a tiny piece of hope buried deep inside me, the same piece of hope that made me love Narnia as a child, that hoped for fairies, that found solace in horses.

That same one lights up like a flickering bulb on a Christmas tree at the sight of the first drunken, red-suited idiot and thinks maybe, just maybe, he is real.

DUCK DUCK GOOSE

My mother loves to tell me the story of my birth. As a kid, every year, I'd be like, "Mom, please no, because I know this story, also it's boring, also can we not?" She'd respond with "The night you were born there was a full moon . . ."

She also loved to tell the tale about how, en route to the hospital, when she was mid-labor, my father was craving French fries and made my mother wait, screaming through her contractions, while he whipped through the McDonald's drive-through to pick up some classic deep-fried finger potatoes. Both of my parents like to . . . embellish, so whether this is true or not, I will never know. But as they say, never let the truth get in the way of a good story.

Other than the McDonald's stop, I think my birth was pretty run-of-the-mill. On the way home my parents stopped off to weigh me on the sugar scale at the local bakery, Rainbow Sweets. My parents were good friends with the owner, who was exactly what you'd expect for a Vermont baker. He was jolly and a little salty when he wanted to be and he baked like a goddamn god.

This all sounds cute and sweet and quaint, doesn't it?

Yeah, it started out nice.

Before my first birthday my parents had divorced. I have zero recollection of them ever being together, and trying to imagine them as a happily married unit is like trying to wrap your head around Anna Wintour doing manual labor. Having them in the same room at my wedding (probably for the first time since they separated) felt like holding a lit cigarette over a lake of gasoline. Nothing like family to make you feel like you're living life on the edge.

By the age of one I was splitting my time between my parents' households. Life was still pretty good as far as I could tell. The back-and-forth sucked, but I was a kid, so I rolled with it. I loved our house in Cambridge. I loved my preschool. I loved my two best friends, Sam and Francesca. (I especially loved Sam, who I had already agreed to marry and procreate with.) I loved when my nanny would take me to the butcher, where he would give me a raw hot dog that I would gobble up. (To this day it is beyond my comprehension that he gave them to me, that my nanny let me eat them, and that I didn't die from those things.) I loved the weather in Cambridge, I loved the fall and the winter and watching the flowers grow in the spring. For a small child, I have a shocking amount of incredibly vivid memories from this time in my life, I think because I was happy.

And then, when I turned five, my mother, my sister, and I moved to Los Angeles.

I started first grade in LA, at a private Christian school in Pacific Palisades. The uniforms were made out of the same material that they make dog leashes from. No matter what the weather, the last Friday of every month we had to wear our "nice" uniforms, which consisted of thick, long-sleeve white button-downs, our dog-leash skirts, tights, and wool sweaters. Otherwise we'd be given detention. I remember dripping sweat in the ninety-plus-degree heat in June, dreaming of the last school bell and being able to rip that sweater off my body. I also remember, in religion class once a week, when the thousand-year-old nun would tell us that if we didn't accept Jesus as our lord and savior we were going to rot in hell. She said this to children, also forgetting or ignoring the fact that there were two Jews in her class, me included. I remember the gym teacher who would ask us every morning, "Hey kids, what did you have for breakfast?" And before we could answer he'd scream, "I EAT NAILS FOR BREAKFAST!"

I also remember my classmates.

To this day, I wonder if they all turned out to be sociopaths or serial killers or dentists, because there was something seriously wrong with them. I spent six years and one week at that school, and I'd rather have my eyelashes pulled off one by one than ever go back and repeat a single hour at that place. "Bullying" honestly feels like too childish a term to describe what I experienced there.

I was an easy target—a strange kid. Not pull-the-wings-off-bugs strange but would-rather-talk-to-horses-than-people-and-believed-in-Santa-Claus-for-far-too-long kinda strange. I was awkward and sad having just been ripped from my friends and moved across the country. I was easily scared and anxious; I got stomachaches and had eczema between my fingers. I loved horses and My Little Pony. I wasn't allowed to watch TV. I still slept with my teddy bear. My incredibly thick hair was cut into a short bob that resembled more of a helmet than a haircut. I wore backwards hats and puka shell necklaces. I rolled my socks down instead of folding them over. I sported bright orange board shorts and shirts from the Delia's catalog that had things like plastic glitter flowers on them, which would have been cute on anyone else but were really just the nails in the coffin of my fashion disaster.

There were many variables that transpired to make me this way, but the main takeaway is, kids are herd animals, and if you smell different, if you scare them, if you are confusing, you threaten the herd.

I was other, and therefore, I had to be removed.

It started early.

I had always been afraid to go to the bathroom alone for fear that when I was helpless, skirt down around my ankles, the monsters I was convinced were hiding in the vacant stalls would come and eat me, or maybe a serial killer would make me his next victim. Compounding it, however, were the boys at that school, who would secretly follow me into the bathroom, wait until they knew I had popped a squat, and then start banging on the bathroom door as loudly as they could. I peed on myself more times than I'd like to admit from that particular game they played.

The mind games were also pretty epic. Once, as I was leaving school, they asked me if I was going to make it to Evie's birthday party. When I responded by asking when it was, they told me to call Evie and ask because she wasn't sure yet. So I called Evie and said, "Hey, Evie, I heard you're having a birthday party. When is it? I'd love to come." At which point Evie burst into hysterical sobs and hung up the phone. A few minutes later, I got a conference call from of a group of girls who berated me for ruining Evie's surprise birthday party.

They made fun of my eczema. They terrorized me when I ran into them trick-or-treating. They scoffed at the clothes that I got to wear on "free dress" day. They invited me to sleepovers only to ignore me the entire time. They called me ugly and dumb and stupid. Bullying me was sport for them and I swear they fucking loved it.

Their crowning achievement came during fifth grade.

I was getting something out of my locker when one of the boys in my class came up to me and pushed me from behind.

"How could you do that to Evie and Marty?! What is wrong with you?" he said. "Honestly, you're sick."

I looked behind him to see the two girls he was referring to: Evie and Marty, tiny, blond, petite, perfect, clutching each other and crying their eyes out.

I told him I didn't know what he was talking about.

And then more boys showed up. And then the rest of the girls showed up. There were forty-two kids in my class. Just enough to create something of a mob but small enough to keep everyone on the same page. Once they had all assembled around me they started yelling things at me about how sick and twisted I was, how disgusting, how cruel.

I just stood there, totally frozen with fear. I had absolutely no idea what they were talking about, but whatever it was, I knew it was not going to end well for me. As they continued to spit names and threats at me—pervert, psycho, sicko, we're gonna get you for this, I'm never inviting you over again, nobody likes you, everybody hates you, eat dirt—I stood there, totally overwhelmed and trying to process what was happening. At first I tried to ask someone to explain, to tell me what they were talking about, that whatever it was I didn't do it. But eventually I just decided to play dead. I gave up and let their attacks wash over me knowing that at some point somebody would come and stop it.

Eventually our teacher showed up and intervened. She took aside one of the students, who apparently explained to her what was going on, and I was escorted to the principal's office.

Our principal was a man in his sixties with a very lovely head of thick white hair. I had always thought he was sweet. But when I walked in he could barely look at me. He spewed some canned speech about how this was a Christian school and we have values to uphold and what could possibly possess me to do such a thing, blah blah blah. When I told him I had no idea what he was talking about, he looked at me like I was a kid with chocolate all over their face swearing they didn't eat the chocolate bar. When I continued to hold firm that I had no idea what he was talking about, he laid it out for me.

Evie and Marty had been found crying on the side of the field during

PE. They were apparently both sobbing hysterically. (I didn't see this.) As girls and boys alike went up to them to see what was going on, they told them apprehensively (yeah, okay, well-played, girls) that I had been going around telling anyone who would listen that at their sleepover the previous weekend they had gone down on each other.

Remember, we were in fifth grade. I didn't even know what that meant yet. Oral sex was not remotely on my ten-year-old radar. Eventually everyone in the class had made their way to Evie and Marty's crying corner and heard the story about this rumor they claimed I'd been spreading about them. And then the group set out to find me, which they did, berated me about what a horrible person I was, and got me sent to the principal's office.

I tried to convince him that the girls were lying and I hadn't started the rumor, that I didn't even know what that was. His response was, "But, Zosia, it's your word against all of theirs."

Every single one of my thirty-nine other classmates had all corroborated Evie and Marty's story, saying they'd heard me spreading this rumor, that I had come up to each and every one of them and not only told them that this had happened but had shared salacious details.

I was sent home for the day. I wasn't expelled or suspended; I think it was just that nobody wanted to look at me for a while.

I always wondered, Why me? Yes, I was an easy target, but it wasn't like every other child at this school was a fucking hot rock star. There was a kid who would pick his nose, put the booger he had picked onto a piece of tape, and tape it to the leg of his desk. He'd do this every day, and the ones that had been there for days or weeks, marinating like a fine wine? He'd eventually rip off and eat as snacks. I mean, why not him?

Why me?

I guess I was the lucky one.

I stayed at that school until a week into my seventh-grade year, when I couldn't take it any longer. The pain and terror and despair I felt getting out of the car every morning for drop-off became too much to take. After six years of pushing through and gritting my teeth and making it through the day in that hellhole, I just ran out of fight, so I dropped out.

I wish that I could say that there was one last big moment giving me the confidence I needed to tell everyone why I refused to go back, but sadly there wasn't. I just finally got up the courage to say no more—something I should have done after my first year there. But I didn't. The years went on and the bullying continued and the loneliness overwhelmed me and yet I still stayed.

But finally, after that week of seventh grade, I knew that if I spent one more day in that school with those kids, I wouldn't make it. It was me or them, and if I stayed it would be them.

I wasn't able to easily begin school anywhere else, so I was home-schooled and then started at a new school in eighth grade, which came with its own trials and tribulations. (I honestly think I'm not cut out for a structured learning environment with other people my age. I always seemed to turn into the wounded, bleeding animal in the water with sharks circling.)

Years later, after I had created a life far, far away from all of those nasty memories, I was doing a play in New York. As I was leaving the theater one night, the security guard stopped me and said that during the performance someone had left a note for me.

It was a letter from Evie. She and her father were visiting New York and she had seen my name on the marquee. "We're so proud of you, Zoshie!" she'd written.

I was immediately that tiny girl again, standing by my locker surrounded by screaming children telling me what a disgusting monster I was, while Evie, standing in the corner, watched it all go down.

I ripped her note into as many pieces as I possibly could, threw them onto the dirty New York sidewalk, and crushed them into the cement with my boot. She had conveniently forgotten that she tried to ruin my life. She didn't get to be proud of me.

I'm sure a lot of people would say that the bullying "made me who I am today," which, okay, sure. It's a thing that happened to me for a prolonged period of time, so of course it's going to mold who I am to a certain extent. But I don't like to think about it that way.

I like to think about it like this: Those kids were monsters. I hope one day Evie and Marty are gunning for big promotions at whatever high-ranking, boring-ass corporate jobs they landed themselves in and their reputations get falsely smeared the way they falsely smeared mine.

You might say that's holding a grudge.

I'd say that's clenching it with both fists and hanging on tight.

I REALLY SHOULDN'T
TELL YOU BUT...

My older sister and I are six years apart, which is exactly the wrong amount apart. I was never close enough in age to understand what she was going through or have anything in common, but I wasn't young enough to be a doll for her to play with. I was basically just utterly annoying to her at all times no matter what I was doing, including if I was in my room sleeping.

As older siblings go, she loved to fuck with me. All in good fun. Although she would hold me down and tickle me until I wet myself, which gave me such PTSD that to this day if someone so much as mentions tickling me I scream. She used to tell me if I stuck my tongue out for too long it would shrivel up and fall off. If I crossed my eyes they'd never go back. She once accidentally gave me a black eye with a tape recorder. When we stayed with our father she'd shove her vegetables onto my plate when nobody was looking and say, "I finished my veggies but Zosia hasn't eaten any of hers!" Sibling shit. But other than the bladder-releasing tickling attacks, it wasn't so bad.

Unlike my little child troll self, my sister was beautiful and popular. I looked like a short, stout, overweight trucker with chopped brown hair and a backwards baseball cap and sinus issues and eczema between my fingers that made my hands look like lizard scales. She looked like a fairy sprite with long shiny golden-blond hair and blue eyes. Unlike my loner self she had a Rolodex of friends. Whenever one of them came over, the desperation to hang out with them, to be a part of their play, to have them include me, was all-encompassing. I would linger outside her door for hours hoping that she would ask me to come in. I'd try to interject myself, coming to the door with a puzzle, or my Breyer horses, or towels for the pool suggesting a swim, only to have her look at me with disgust and slam the door in my face, and then she and her friends would giggle loud enough behind the door that I could hear them laughing at my expense.

But one time, the unthinkable happened. She came into my room with her friend and told me she had a secret that she absolutely should not but absolutely must share with me. I thought that I had won the lottery. I thought that my world was finally opening up and all the dreams that I had wished for on every eyelash I could pluck out of my tiny eyelid were finally coming true.

I should have known it wasn't real by their unsuccessful attempts to suppress the giddy laughter bubbling out of them. But I was seven and my sister and her friends were thirteen and I didn't stand a chance.

"We have to tell you something, but you absolutely cannot tell another living soul about this, okay?! We should not be telling you this and we could get in such massive trouble for it but we thought you had a right to know."

I waited with bated breath as they looked at each other, faces red with barely held-back laughter. What were they going to share? My tiny brain was too excited to even dare to imagine.

"Okay, PINKY SWEAR you will not tell another living soul about this, okay!"

I, obviously, pinky swore.

And then, I can honestly say, without a shadow of a doubt, that I never would have guessed what came out of their mouths.

"So, when you turn thirteen, you get a penis."

My tiny mind exploded.

I opened my mouth and ten thousand questions spilled out.

"How do they give it to you?"

"In a ceremony."

"Where do you keep it?"

"In an ornamental box."

"Do they teach you how to use it?"

"Yes."

"Is it detachable?"

"Obviously."

"Do you keep it forever?"

"Duh."

"Why thirteen?"

"We don't know, don't ask dumb questions."

This was news. I mean this was BIG news. The fact that she was sharing a secret of this magnitude with me? I mean, it was everything I'd ever wanted.

But as the excitement of this initial acceptance into her inner sanctum started to wear off, logic began to creep in. Of course, I wanted proof. So I asked to see her penis.

"We can't show you ours! We've already told you too much! If we show you they'll for sure know and we'll get ours taken away!"

I begged them to show me, I pleaded with them. They refused. I told them I wouldn't believe them unless they showed me. And then they did the worst thing of all. They said, "Fine, we don't care if you believe us or not," and they started to walk away.

I had to keep them around. I had to keep this newfound bonding experience going.

"WAIT!" I screamed after them. "I believe you, I believe you!"

My sister looked at me sympathetically. In my recollection she stroked the side of my face lovingly, but I know that's an embellishment my memory added later for dramatic effect and desire for her warmth. But the sympathetic look was real. Although, honestly, it also could have just been pity. Either way she looked at me and said, "Look, if you don't believe me, go ask Mom."

Duh! How could I have been so utterly stupid! Mom! Of course Mom would show me hers! And I could get all my questions answered. What a jolly day! So I ran off into the hallway screaming so loudly that I couldn't hear my sister's victorious cackling laughter over me: "Mom!!!! Mom!!!!!!!! Will you show me your penis?!"

CRACKED

Growing up, I was afraid of drugs.

I was too terrified of psychedelics to so much as be in the same room as them.

Nobody started doing ecstasy or Molly or acid until college, so that wasn't something I had to actively avoid.

And I knew cocaine's side effect of quelling hunger, not to mention the energy boost, would be incredibly appealing to my anorexic mind, so I steered clear. At the time, I was so malnourished, the possibility of it giving me the energy I so desperately lacked? I would have fucking loved cocaine! So I stayed away.

My steadfast refusal is ironic, given the fact that when I was young, my anxiety was so bad, every morning felt like the fresh hell of waking up a nut inside a nutcracker. You'd think I would have run to drugs like an old lady to a BOGO at the grocery store. But for some reason the idea of numbing the anxiety always sounded more terrifying to me than simply sitting in it like a hot bathtub of unease. The devil you know, I guess . . .

But as a California kid, the one drug it was hard to get away from was pot. (At least the brilliance of peer pressure made it feel that way.) So I smoked it occasionally, never enjoying it or truly feeling the fantastic effects that all my peers raved about. During those moments, my friends would be laughing uncontrollably, seemingly living their best lives, dancing on tables and ravenously shoving candy into their mouths. Meanwhile, I huddled in a corner trying to regulate my breathing and remind myself that someday I would feel normal again.

And that's all I did, other than incessant drinking, until one day at a house party out in Malibu, I accidentally smoked crack.

I was sixteen. It was a Saturday. One of my classmates had a beach house out on a private road in Malibu. When it isn't the height of summer and the owners are enjoying their other homes across the city, those beach neighborhoods feel like ghost towns. You walk down the beach, which is essentially the backyard of every house, and in place of other humans you get seagulls. Not to say that if you saw humans, they'd be particularly neighborly in this section of the world. Even though the houses are literally stacked on top of one another, there is an unspoken agreement: I have paid an exorbitant amount of money for this slice of my personal paradise. You stay on your side and let's pretend the other one doesn't exist. All that to say, it doesn't exactly feel like you could go and knock on your next-door neighbors' door in an emergency.

My friend's parents were away for the week, so she graciously offered to throw a rager at her beach house for the entire grade. Parties always made me nervous. The idea of being in a room surrounded by people who knew how to let go, how to enjoy themselves, how to do whatever they wanted without caring what other people thought, not to mention having to attempt to emulate that in a way that would make them believe I was one of them, was like being in my own personal horror film. But in an effort to not seem like the outcast that I felt like inside, I went and put on a smile and pretended to have fun.

I wasn't unpopular in high school. I wasn't popular either. I had a core group of friends who I loved. But I was lost. I came into high school with a steamer trunk's worth of emotional baggage and PTSD from the elementary school I'd had to flee because the bullying got so bad. If you polled people I'd gone to high school with, they'd probably say they loved me. I say that not to sound arrogant but to paint a picture that I think I was a likable human in high school. But if you'd asked me in high school what people thought of me, I would have told you the majority of those people hated me and thought I was an annoying loser. Just getting dressed in the mornings before school made me want to throw up. Granted, I went to an incredibly ritzy Hollywood high school where some of my classmates never so much as repeated a pair of shoes twice in their entire four years there, so getting dressed did come with an added bit of pressure. I was big on magical thinking at the time: If I could just wear the perfect outfit, everyone would like me. And if I wore the wrong outfit . . . well. I was smart and funny and cool, and yet my crippling insecurity told me otherwise. And so I hid within and starved myself.

But I still went to the party. Anyone else who has gone to high school can tell you that not going is far, far worse than going and having a bad time. I feel like the slogan for high school overall should be "Grin and bear it till graduation."

This time I really tried. I bought the booze with my fake ID at the local Ralphs. Standing in that checkout line, pushing a shopping cart filled to the brim with cheap vodka and mixers, I could feel the sweat gathering in my armpits as the cashier ran my ID. When she handed me my receipt, I felt like I'd just rigged the lottery and won. (To this day, I'm still convinced I racked up some sort of karmic debt that day in getting away with it.)

When I arrived, the music was blaring, and the blender was going a mile a minute churning out frozen margaritas. The weather was perfect and the beach was pristine. There must have been a hundred kids in that beach house. What could possibly go wrong?

As I attempted to dance like a normal person, masking the tension I felt in every one of my cells, my friend handed me a joint. And as always, not wanting them to know I was an imposter, I took it. And I smoked the entire thing, hoping that the weed would numb my brain enough to possibly, just maybe, for once, actually have a good time.

Sadly, that's not what happened.

The girl throwing the party had a cousin who at the time we all thought was endlessly cool. In his twenties, he seemed so old and worldly, forging his own path in the world doing what he wanted. (In retrospect, I can now see he was a loser who had dropped out of high school and was dealing bad overpriced drugs to teenagers.)

This cousin had supplied the drugs for the party. And what I wouldn't find out until the next day was that the joint I smoked wasn't just pot—it was pot laced with crack.

About twenty minutes after I smoked the joint I started to feel strange. The noise of the blender was what kicked it off—all of a sudden, it felt like the metal blade had crawled inside my eardrums and was hacking away at the tissue. I kept checking my ears to make sure they weren't bleeding. The pain got so bad that I went outside to sit on the beach hoping for some sort of respite.

I ran into a couple of friends out on the sand who couldn't stop laughing. Their laughter felt like knives being jammed in quick succession into every part of my body, like my entire being was covered in gashes every time they so much as giggled. It was so painful I could barely catch my breath.

That's when I knew I was in trouble.

The drugs transported me into an alternate reality, like a bad DJ had taken over the controls and was remixing the information as it entered my brain. The sounds around me slowed, then sped up to the pace of a chipmunk with ADHD. Then they went beyond to a decibel only dogs could hear. The changes continued in an uneven loop, never stopping for a second to normalize, making me dizzy.

Then the visuals began. It was like a John Waters movie on rewind with bad eighties transitions. I was sitting, staring at my friends laughing, and suddenly they were right in front of my face, close and blown up, as if they'd rushed at me at full speed. And then they became tiny dots a thousand miles away, specks of existence surrounded by blackness.

I was hit with vibrant colors and sound, and then everything would go black. No sound, no sight. The whiplash made me sick. Each time the sound rushed back in, the pain felt more unbearable, escalating to a point where I thought my head was going to pop off my neck.

There was nobody to help, nobody to calm me down or tell me this was just a bad trip or give me some Gatorade or hold me as I convulsed with fear. Because everyone else had smoked the same tainted weed. Everyone else was cracked out of their faces. And everyone else was fucking loving it.

I stumbled away from my friends, whose cackles I thought would eventually kill me, and found a spot on the sand that felt far away from everyone. As I sat there, staring at the waves coming in and going out in rhythmic succession, I felt defeat wash over me. This is my life now, I thought to myself. This is what existence feels like. You will never feel normal again. Welcome to hell, your new home.

Eventually I made my way to my car and figured out how to shove myself into the space underneath the steering wheel. I hid there like a scared animal burrowing into a hole. It took me about two hours but I somehow figured out how to call my boyfriend at the time. He hated the fact that I smoked pot. (Funnily enough, I'd find out much later on that he had been the coke dealer for our entire school and every other private school within a ten-mile radius, so he was a bit of a hypocrite. He was also a pretty massive asshole and an angry drunk.)

When I got him on the phone, I stammered out what was happening. To which he responded, "Don't call me when you're high." And then he hung up on me.

There was no one else to call. All my friends were at the party, their brains deliciously melting down the backs of their throats, making them incapable of helping me in my time of need. Obviously, I couldn't call my parents or go to the hospital. At that age you'd rather die than get in trouble. I couldn't knock on a neighbor's door because, as we've established, they either weren't there or would be so bothered that I'd ruined their Saturday off at the beach house that they wouldn't help.

So I stayed shoved underneath my steering wheel for five hours.

Eventually I gathered up enough courage and decided to drive myself home. I know now this was one of the worst things I ever could have done, but at the time, the need to be in my own bed outweighed the fear of driving while high off my face on crack weed.

I pulled the seat of my car so far up to the steering wheel that I could just fit my body inside. I looked like one of those little grandmas who should have had their licenses revoked years ago but were somehow still driving themselves to bingo night. I drove down PCH at the exact speed limit the entire way home, terrified that if I went too slow or even slightly too fast, the state troopers parked out along the highway would know my dirty little secret, pull me over, and put me away for life.

After what felt like hours but was probably more like forty-five minutes, I made it home. I had gripped the steering wheel so hard, I had to pry my fingers off one by one.

My parents were away, and the silence of the house felt like a glorious sensory deprivation chamber compared to the horror of stimulation I had just come from. I crawled into my bed and stared at the ceiling shaking until I eventually fell asleep.

The hangover the next day was exceptional. I'd never experienced anything quite like it. And I'm almost reticent to call it a hangover because I think I was high for another day or so. It was as if the drugs were still in my bloodstream, taking their sweet old time down the lazy river.

After the high finally wore off, I walked around in a heavy daze. My brain was muted and dull like I had used up my senses and had to wait for them to replenish before I could experience life at full tilt again. It took a solid week for me to feel any semblance of normalcy.

My friend's cousin called the next day to apologize to her. He said he'd given her the wrong drugs. That was weed with a kick. He hoped everyone had a good time.

I think everyone else did. I doubt any of us would have sought out crack at the time, but my classmates seemed to enjoy themselves. But what was just another weekend house party to them was, or at least felt like, a near-death experience to me.

I didn't smoke pot for a decade after that. I was too afraid, the memory of that experience seared into my brain.

Years later, I had to film an episode of *Girls* where I accidentally smoke crack at a party and absolutely lose my mind. The episode was called "The Crackcident," fittingly so. Almost nobody knew about my own little teenage crackcident so the fact that it was written for my character was total happenstance.

I didn't tell anybody about my past experience at the time. I was still too ashamed and embarrassed. But as we were shooting, a couple of the crew members were saying things like, "Damn, you seem to be nailing this reaction! You sure you haven't smoked crack before?" I would giggle and make a funny face and change the subject.

A bad trip is fucking horrific. Anyone who has had one to any degree can attest to the fact that when you're in it you feel like you're dying and that it's never going to end. The residue this leaves can last for years, maybe even your whole life. When it happened to me, I remember thinking, Why me? I follow the rules, I don't do anything too crazy, I'm already anxious as a fucking mouse in a cat's litter box, why the fuck did this happen to me?

But filming that episode is probably the most fun I've ever had at work. And the catharsis was incredible. Taking an experience that had been so horrifying, that had scared me for years, and being able to use it toward something good and funny and ridiculous?

It almost made it worth it.

I'D KILL FOR YOUR KNEES

I am at the Soho House in Los Angeles eavesdropping.

"It has to be Will Smith or we're not making it," a self-proclaimed "very important" producer says at the table next to me. (You know someone's a hack when they wear sunglasses inside. As if everybody else can't see that they are quite literally trying to hide the all-encompassing insecurity that they will eventually be found out as utter bullshit.) The other guys at the table nod in stern agreement. Will Smith or bust.

At the table next to them, a doe-eyed girl trying to give off sexy-single-mom vibes in an attempt to hide her I'm-a-teenage-runaway vibes gazes in a moony way at the much older man sitting with her, maybe her agent? "Trust me, babe. I've been doing this a long time. Take the time to get your nose and tits done NOW before we introduce you to the world. You only get one first impression." And then he starts sounding off names of plastic surgeons she should reach out to. She gobbles up the lies like candy.

At the table next to *them*, an overly tanned older man brags to seemingly nobody, "Oh, honey, I've done everyone's hair. Fucked 'em, chopped their split ends, done lines off their dicks. You name 'em I've done 'em top to bottom."

But for the most part, it's all a scam. One huge fucking scam. That table of men casually throwing around Will Smith's name? They are probably never gonna make a movie in their lives.

That teenage girl? She'll maybe get a bit part on a shitty network show or become an extra for a few years before she ends up doing porn in the Valley.

And that hairdresser? He probably did one famous guy's hair, or maybe it was just someone that looked like a famous guy, twenty years ago, and now he works at Supercuts.

Every day, the cacophony of bullshit swells like a swarm of bees. All these humans living in this city deluding themselves into buying their own snake oil, because none of them feel like they're enough—not famous enough, not pretty enough, not rich enough.

Now imagine being a teenager in this acid-trip environment.

Then imagine being a teenage girl in this environment.

I think it's safe to say that growing up in Los Angeles, none of us girls ever felt good enough. Well, at least I personally never felt good enough, but in hindsight I'm pretty sure it was the entire tribe. There was always some way you could be better, skinnier, more fashionable, funnier, more aloof, more desirable, smarter—you name it, there was always room for improvement. But of course perfection was elusive. I always felt like I was sent out on a treasure hunt without clues or hints or an end goal in sight—I just knew I was on the hunt and that if I came back empty-handed, I would be shunned for all eternity. I mean, what a joy, right? (There isn't enough money in the world to tempt me to relive my teenage years.)

We girls needed each other in order to feel safe, in order to understand what was happening to and around us. But at the same time, that companionship felt more like the Hunger Games. We all knew the rules: there is not enough love for all of us, we will not all make it, there are those who are better and those who are lesser, and the divide must be clear.

I was not good at playing the game, but as it wasn't optional, I played the best I could: by hiding instead of trying to win.

I was born with a deep insecurity chip inside my brain, perhaps a factory malfunction, that only grew more pronounced in my teen years. As the rest of the girls shuffled through different versions of themselves, figuring out what they liked and didn't, I followed the motions, but I never ended up with conclusive data. My page continued to hold a question mark.

The one thing I felt helped on this road to self-discovery was the approval of other girls (not the boys, they weren't the important ones). Unlike some of my peers, I didn't see other girls as competition or want to take them down the way others might. (Perhaps that's another part of me that doesn't work properly. Darwin would have something to say about that—too soft, I would have died in the wild.) No, I just wanted them to love me.

I usually had an insecurity siren screaming in my head, "YOU DON'T KNOW WHO YOU ARE! EVERYONE CAN TELL! NOBODY LIKES YOU! IF BEIGE WERE A PERSON THAT WOULD BE YOU!" But if another girl told me she liked my shirt or laughed at my joke, it was like that scene in *Pleasantville* when the character wakes up, going from a black-and-white world to one with color. Their approval solidified me as a person with opinions and desires and direction. But because teenage girls are not the most giving, these moments of approval were few and far between. And unfortunately, the high from any compliment wore off quickly, and then I'd be back to my beige self, hunting for an approval fix to define my personality.

In the midst of all this, I managed to just barely graduate from high school. I say "barely" because I couldn't pass algebra, and because each year I very nearly dropped out. By the time I got to senior year, I was so angry that I'd wasted four years of my life sitting in those horrifically uncomfortable chairs (probably the reason I have back problems today), listening to my teachers drone on about shit I was going to forget in six months anyway. But there we were. I'd gotten to the end of the line and somehow, I crossed over. I got my diploma. I was officially a high school graduate. Yippee.

Once my school days were behind me, it wasn't all sunshine and rainbows. But I loved the freedom of not being in school. Not getting up early, not having homework, not constantly being under the judging glare of my peers . . . those were perks for sure. I'd still have the occasional classic dream where I'd wake up drenched in sweat, terrified that I'd forgotten my final essay for social studies, but I'd feel so much relief when I remembered that I'd graduated six weeks before and I'd never have to do homework again.

Granted, I was a little lonely. Everyone else I'd known had gone off to college and was consumed with creating their new personas within their brand-new lives. And here I was at home, pursuing acting: learning pages and pages of sides for endless auditions I wouldn't get and spending my evenings reading books in bed or going to movies by myself. But despite my loneliness, I was mostly happy.

Maybe this was because once I was out of school, I had discovered I no longer needed the validation of other girls to affirm who I was and what I liked. That instinct had been packed away and sent off with former classmates to various sorority houses around the country. And I hadn't so much as missed it. Not having them around forced me to sit with myself and wonder, What do I like and want and feel? I still don't have a fully-fledged answer to that question, but at the time, I actually started to find myself a bit more, discovering happiness where before there had only been a fanny pack full of anxiety and crippling insecurity.

I finally admitted to myself that I hated partying and staying out late. So I traded in my platform bootie heels for my father's oversized wool socks and started doing what I actually wanted in the evening:

getting into bed in the single-digit hours. Without the pressure of my peers scanning my phone for "recently played" in my iTunes, I found out that even though my taste in music is eclectic and, I'd like to think, not horrible, pop music is something I enjoy. So I began listening to Kelly Clarkson and Robyn and Pink unironically. My love for thrifting, which had lain dormant given that "vintage" was a dirty word to the girls I went to school with, finally bloomed and I spent endless hours in the Goodwills and Salvation Armies of Los Angeles. It felt like the first time in my life that I wasn't being graded on my personhood. So I began to live as if it wasn't a test.

And then winter break came around, and everyone flocked home for the holidays. I was invited to a house party thrown by one of the beautiful popular girls I'd gone to school with. I knew the party would be populated with all the other beautiful popular girls from high school—the ones I had tried to emulate and impress and gain approval from, the ones I had spent the last few months detangling myself from.

As I picked out my outfit for the party, my old anxiety and insecurity tugged at the loose ends of the self-assurance sweater I had been knitting around myself. I tried to remind myself that I was my own person, that their opinion of me was just that, an opinion. That I didn't need them . . . right?

I wish.

Knowing I was going to see them put me right back to square one. It was almost Pavlovian. I immediately began trying to think like them again, to anticipate what they would want from me, how they would judge me, how to please them. I found myself yet again in the cycle of desperately needing their stamp of approval. I filtered through what I had been reading and watching and listening to, trying to predict if they would like it or not. Was that a cool enough band, album, book, movie? If it wasn't cool enough, was it uncool in a way that they would consider interestingly ironic? I weighed every part of my existence against what their judgment of it would be. I agonized about what to wear, and while I don't remember what outfit I landed on, I do remember hating whatever I'd picked by the time I showed up.

The evening was nice enough. We all drank wine and pretended to be the grown-ups we thought we had become. I heard about everyone's college experiences. How cold they all were in their various East Coast locales. How hard finals had been. How cute the boys were.

They asked me questions like I was something from a nature documentary. How did I spend my time? Had my parents regretted not forcing me to go? They gushed over how lucky I was that I didn't have to write term papers or attend boring gen-ed classes. But they also made it clear that I was on the outside, that they all shared something I wasn't a part of.

It was interesting, though. Their demarcation was clear: We are college students and you are not. You don't understand the things we are talking about, things like dorms and midterms and rush week. But for the first time ever, it didn't make me feel bad, because for the first time ever I could sense that being different wasn't something they looked down upon but something they were actually intrigued by. I had done something they couldn't comprehend, and in doing so had become something they were curious about. It scared me a little bit, because I knew that this interest could quickly turn to dislike if they decided my choices weren't ones they approved of, but for the moment it felt good. I had their attention. I held it gently and inhaled.

Later that night, I was sitting around a low table with a couple of girls and the queen bee of our former high school class was sitting across from me. She was looking at me with an expression that I couldn't decode.

My brain went to all the usual awful places: She hates me, she thinks I'm ugly, she despises my outfit, she's gonna ask me why I was always such a loser in high school. I'd gotten too comfortable and now they were turning on me.

But then she said, "You have. The most. Amazing knees." And I realized that the expression on her face was one I didn't recognize because I'd never seen it before. She was looking at me with envy.

Her eyes went down to my knees and lingered there. It wasn't sexual or even sensual; it was more like a hunger. I think if she could have chopped off my knees and put them onto her own she would have.

"I would kill to have knees like that," she continued. "The way they go in at the sides. My knees are just one big blob. I have fat knees. You have such beautiful skinny knees. I would fucking kill to have your knees."

The lust in her eyes scared me. But at the same time I could feel the void inside me filling up like a helium balloon at a party store. I knew it wouldn't sustain me for long, but her jealousy made me feel worthy, wanted, better-than, in a way I never had before.

As I suspected, the high did not last. And as the dopamine surge of approval wore off I realized something incredibly sad: that even though I had started to find myself, that I thought I had started to grow beyond the need for their acceptance, I hadn't. Getting it still mattered just as much, it still felt just as good.

I'd like to say that I have since grown beyond it entirely now but I'd be lying. The pot never feels entirely full and there is always room for more, and every time the current version of an LA teen girl casts their stamp of approval upon me, tells me I'm talented, or funny, or skinny, or stylish, my body swells with the same high it did as an insecure teen. The fix will always be as good, and some part of me will always want it. Some part of me will, truthfully, always need it. Maybe that's part of why I became an actor, a profession where I am constantly searching for the outward approval of others.

But hey, apparently, I've got great knees. I've never forgotten that moment. And sometimes when I'm feeling particularly down about myself I think, Well, Riley would kill to have my knees, and that, at least, buys me a couple minutes of reprieve from the monkeys in my brain.

BOO

Imagine you go to get ice cream but you can't decide on a flavor, so you convince the super high kid working the counter to let you shove four different flavors into a medium cup, and then you lose your mind with toppings: sprinkles, gummy bears, carob chips (because you're being healthy), crumbled Oreo cookies. You leave the ice cream shop after having paid twelve dollars for your ice cream. And as you look down, excited to dig in, you see what you're left with: a melting Frankenstein mosh pit of inedible milky insanity.

Now imagine instead of ice cream and toppings in that cup, it's all neuroses: self-hatred, insecurity, social anxiety, body dysmorphia.

That, ladies and gentlemen, was what my brain was like as a teenager.

I'm not entirely sure where along my timeline as a budding human it began, but somewhere in between being born and becoming self-aware, I developed a pretty significant sense of worthlessness. By the time I was twenty I had little to no self-respect and was shocked when any boy who was remotely attractive and not (seemingly) a serial killer so much as looked at me.

It's hard to say how much of this was a self-fulfilling prophecy. Looking back, a lot of it could have been. But either way, I wasn't getting much attention from anyone. Man, woman, child, animal. It was almost as if I were invisible. At the time, I was attempting to starve myself into a black hole, but even while I was on that path I still wanted someone to love me and tell me I was pretty. Isn't that what we all want? But whether I was a ghost, or physically unappealing, or my aura was too thick with anxiety for others to see through, no boy wanted to touch me, literally or metaphorically.

So when I was twenty and a hot boy hit on me at a hot nightclub on a hot Saturday night, at first I thought maybe Ashton Kutcher was hiding behind the bar. But then again, I wasn't special or famous enough to be on an episode of *Punk'd*. So then I thought maybe there had just been a mistake. Perhaps the boy was blind or confused or doing research for his thesis paper about hitting on unworthy women to see what their reaction might be.

I'm obviously not going to tell you the boy's name, but in order to give you a sense of his vibe, we'll call him Lucas. Does that paint a picture?

Lucas and I had gone to the same high school but he'd graduated a few years before me. We hadn't crossed paths before. I think I became a freshman the year after he'd graduated. But that night, we talk for hours. He buys me glasses of wine. He is self-deprecating in all the right ways. He knows he's attractive but he doesn't gloat about it, and he isn't so hot that you feel uncomfortable in his presence. He's not sweet enough to be the boy next door, but if you throw a pair of glasses on him he'd be that kind of nerdy sexy that only exists in nineties rom-coms. He also makes me laugh. Or, I should say, he seems to want to make me laugh. And he pays attention to me, which is utterly shocking to my self-hating little brain.

On a Saturday night, in this hot-spot club filled with LA starlets, models, and searingly sexy heiresses, for some reason he is paying attention to ME.

When the time comes to leave, he walks me to the door and kisses me. He'd asked for my number earlier in the evening, and after he kisses me he says he'll call me. "I want to take you to dinner," he says.

And then he gives me one of those looks that, again, really only exist in nineties rom-coms, like the look that Sandra Bullock or Meg Ryan gets from the floppy-haired brother (of the leading man) who she's actually in love with. Even though the leading man has more money and better eyebrows, and she thought she was in love with him at first but the ninety-minute movie has now made her fall for the floppy-haired brother.

The look is the relationship equivalent of how people say their life flashes before them when they die. When a guy looks at you like that, you see the next five years in quick succession (only the good stuff, obviously), and it makes you hope just for a moment that maybe you won't be alone forever. You see your first date, and your twentieth date, and meeting his parents, and waking up in his T-shirt and boxer shorts because you slept over by accident. You see dinner with your friends, and moving in together, and a proposal, you see a relationship and a partner, and you think, just for a brief fleeting moment, that maybe you aren't an unattractive broken dumpster fire of a worthless person. Maybe if you faked your own death and ran away to a mountain somewhere in the middle of nowhere, never to be seen or heard from again, people would miss you, people would cry at your funeral. This look makes you think maybe, just maybe, you do indeed deserve love.

So he kisses me, he gives me the look, he says he'll call me. I drive home. I could probably float on the back of a fucking piece of stale bread, I am so high from the evening. I am a water balloon of serotonin bubbles. I am the kid and his grandpa from *Willy Wonka* before shit got dark and they had to burp themselves away from decapitation by that massive fan. I am a dolphin and a rainbow and Christmas morning in human form. I AM LISA FRANK.

I fall asleep that night with a smile on my face and, for the first time in a long time, without the assistance of pharmaceuticals.

I wake up the next morning RENEWED! REJUVENATED! I have a whole new lease on life, I am an entirely different person, I'm no longer insecure or anxious or sad! I'm going to start wearing blouses in pastel colors. I'm going to stop hiding in my room and reading Russian novels by myself most nights. I'm going to start LIVING because I. AM. WORTHY. Because A. BOY. LIKES MEEEEEE!!!!!!!!!!!!

And then . . .

Obviously . . .

He doesn't call.

Days go by.

Weeks go by.

I become obsessed with my phone. I am one with it. It practically becomes an extension of my arm, I hold on to it so frequently and so tight, willing a call or a text or an email to arrive. I work out with it (which, yes, I know isn't that strange, but try doing yoga while holding your phone). I go to the bathroom with it (which, yes, again not THAT strange, but what is strange is that it becomes increasingly hard to have a bowel movement because all I can think about is when he's going to call). I sleep with it clutched in my hand set to vibrate so that if he decides to call I'll feel it and it will wake me out of my slumber. I fucking SHOWER with it. I start to hear phantom noises and am convinced that my phone rang or dinged, and then I am confused when there's still nothing.

I consider learning witchcraft in order to cast a spell to make him call. I consider destroying my phone so I don't have to know whether or not he called. I consider becoming a monk and leaving the world behind so I never have to think about a boy calling ever again. I decide love and relationships and men in general are overrated and unnecessary and that I wouldn't even be happy if someone loved me, what a burden love is, am I right? And I get it, you're thinking, What a fucking crazy person, all he said was "I'll call you." But to anyone who has been out there on the field, you know what I am talking about. You know how the neurosis adds up to create this magical obsessive potpie: the exhaustion of dating, the anxiety fearing you'll be alone forever with a house full of one-eyed cats, the crushing weight of loneliness, the heavy topping of self-hatred, worthlessness, and childhood trauma, and voilà! Your recipe for feeling like actual loser roadkill when a guy who seems like a nice, normal prospect ghosts you.

I become even more of a trash heap of neurotic, insecure limp spaghetti than I was before he cursed me with that fucking side smile / sweet peck on the lips / look of hope / "I'll call you" bullshit. I torture myself like this for too long. I go through all the stages of grief on a circle until I'm dizzy, and I look like that emoji with the squiggle eyeballs. I become a shell of myself. Eventually, I just can't take it anymore. The self-inflicted torture (well, semi-self-inflicted; yes, I made myself crazy about it, but that motherfucker started it when he said he would call me) becomes unbearable and I throw in the towel. Write him off. Give up.

And then . . .

He calls.

The second I decide to give up and admit to myself that he's never going to call. He does. (Well, he texts, but who calls anyone anymore? This was, like, over a decade ago, but still, people only call when there's an emergency or they're your mother.)

(Also, how the FUCK do men know to finally make contact when you've decided you're no longer thinking about them? There has to be a scientific explanation, because it happens every single time. But you can't cheat the system. It doesn't work if you pretend to not be thinking about them. You have to truly, deep inside your soul, decide that you do not care, you will never care, you never really did care if they live or die or call you or want to spend the rest of their life trying to make you happy. You have to stop giving a fuck about them. ZERO fucks. No fucks at all. And the second that you do, the second that you release them from your consciousness, that's when they come running.)

Anyway, he texts. And hope floods back into me like it's been injected straight into my veins. I am well again, I am happy, I am putty in his hands, I will be whatever he wants me to be.

And the text banter begins!

I have no illusions about myself when it comes to dating. I've now been with my husband for thirteen years, so I haven't exactly been out there trying my luck on the field, but you don't forget these things about yourself. And as much as my sweet, sweet husband adores me, I know he would confirm this statement: I have zero. Fucking. Game. I mean, none to speak of. And this isn't me being cute or self-deprecating. I am not good at dating. If there were dating teams like in kickball you would begrudgingly pick me last.

But the one thing I have going for me is that I can banter like a motherfucker. Especially via text. Out the gate, at least. After too long, my spark dies away—I think the pressure of the beginning of something keeps me sharp.

We banter like a well-oiled machine. The quips are quipping, the innuendos are innuendo-ing, it's cute, it's funny, it's all going great. And we're not just talking your good morning / good night text—I am glued to my phone typing away all day every day. I could be a fucking secretary from 1953 with the amount I am typing. And the speed! I mean, don't even get me started on the speed. My fingers are like Marvel superheroes.

This sounds great, you're thinking, right? Well, yes . . . except . . .

every time we get to the point of making a plan to hang out, confirming a time and day, he disappears for a week.

This goes on forever, for too long. I keep thinking, Does this guy just not want to hang out with me? But then he pops up on my phone and texts me nonstop for five days straight and I think, Okay! We get as far as "Want to hang out?" "I'd love to." "How about Saturday?" "Saturday's great, wanna see a movie?"

And then, like clockwork, he goes dark again.

I go with it, because even though this clearly isn't getting off to a super healthy start, what can I say, I like him and want to keep that ember of hope alive. So when he texts, I respond. When he says, "How about Thursday?" I say, "Great, what time?" When he disappears, I just hope that he will return yet again to repeat the cycle.

Until FINALLY.

One fateful day.

We break the cycle.

We make a plan.

And it actually happens.

He takes me to a movie. When he drives me home, he pulls up outside of my house, puts his car in park, and turns it off. He drives a hot-boy BMW sedan. A classic LA chosen-child car. The new milky leather of the seats makes the entire moment feel somehow better, nicer, more. He puts on the Beatles. And we sit there, in his car, on the street outside my house, for hours, listening to those perfect albums and talking.

We are the only two people on the planet. Nobody has ever been happier or more content than us. I am in bliss.

He kisses me. And then we ferociously make out for hours. I think, This is it. Maybe I will finally have a boyfriend who is kind and normal and is not a drug addict and is nice to me. Maybe I won't be alone forever.

Eventually we stop making out and I go inside feeling like the luckiest girl in the world, already thinking about our next date.

Now I'm sure you can all see where this is going. And you're all gonna be right.

The cycle of him going dark when I ask about making plans continues. For a few weeks. Then a few months. Eventually, it stops altogether, and I never see him again.

I am sad, because I really liked the guy, but more than that I am just confused. Why keep putting in the effort to keep me on the hook? Why keep texting, why take me out at all? Why even call me in the first place?

I imagine he has died in a tragic plane crash. He's been kidnapped. He's gone to prison. He's joined a cult.

I finally decide he just wasn't that into me. C'est la vie, life goes on, and all that bullshit. Things are going to be okay. I have a career to think about and anxiety to tend to and an eating disorder that I am still trying to wrangle into submission. Who has time for a boyfriend or love and happiness anyway?

So I let it go and go on with my life. I audition, I party, I try to not think about how much I hate myself. I go to therapy, I read books, I audition more, I spiral into anxiety pits. Days pass, weeks pass, months pass, a year passes.

Then one night I am out with some friends (at a different club this time) and I see him. He is standing across the room. And he looks good. So good.

I hate that I am still attracted to him, and I decide to avoid him at all costs. So I bob and weave throughout the dark club for the rest of the evening, trying to steer clear.

I am waiting for the bartender to give me my drink and am being incredibly discreet, standing to the side of the bar instead of in front of it, when he walks right up to me.

"Hi," he says.

And I melt.

The puppy-dog eyes are on and turned up to full volume.

I hate that those work. I hate that those work on me.

"Hi," I say.

And then he proceeds to give me a full-blown nineties rom-com third-act "I'm sorry, I don't deserve you, please forgive me" speech. He tells me he thinks I am incredible and he adores spending time with me and he thinks I am smart and funny and beautiful and he really likes me. He says he thinks we have something really special, a true connection. He says that right after we stopped talking he got a DUI and then he got sober. He's been sober for almost a year now. He apologizes for how he behaved. He says he was wasted almost all the time and that he was entirely disconnected from the world, not caring how he treated himself or others. He says he knows he doesn't deserve it, but he would do anything if I will consider giving him a second chance. He says he wants to take me to dinner, and will I please, please, please say yes.

This is when he starts crying. He seemed so ashamed, so remorseful, so genuine.

It is amazing.

Obviously, I say yes. The man laid his heart out at my feet and practically begged me to go on a date with him. He told me I was special. He told me he was sorry. This is the shit we all dream of. This is the shit we cling to, in the dead of night when we are in our darkest hour, and all seems lost, and the loneliness feels like a rising tide that is going to drown us slowly. This is the shit that keeps us going.

He kisses me on the cheek and tells me he will call me the next day. As he walks away, swallowed up by the crowd, I feel a smile spread across my face and a warmth seeping through my body and tendriling its way through my veins.

Hope.

I sleep that night without sleeping pills, dreaming of what lies ahead, dreaming of our next date, dreaming of him calling tomorrow.

I never hear from him again.

BUNGALOW 8

I was a pretty straitlaced kid growing up. I was a perfect student, I didn't drink too much, I didn't do any drugs, I didn't miss curfew, I cleaned my room, I got to school on time, I was good. I wasn't born with that rebellious streak, and the idea of pushing boundaries made me sweat. But adolescence is not for the faint of heart, and between the usual run-of-the-mill torture of high school, familial trouble, and a raging eating disorder, I had to turn to something to get me through the jungle of existence. So when I was seventeen, I threw in the towel on my puritan behavior and stepped into the persona of an all-out hellion.

I had a year left on the prison sentence of my academic career. I wasn't applying to college, and having already started auditioning, I was one foot out the door anyway. And I was drinking, a lot—most likely as a way to numb my gnawing self-hatred and the insatiable hunger I felt from starving myself.

I started taking trips to New York.

I'm not sure how I convinced my father, but I suppose my prudish behavior up until that point had bought me enough good karma for him not to question my actions. I'd use the excuse of a meeting, an audition, or better yet, a huge callback. What my father didn't know was that there was no audition, there was no meeting, there wasn't even a potential opportunity. I was going to New York to party myself into a black hole.

I fell in fast with a socialite crowd, sort of a real-life version of *Gossip Girl*—people who were endlessly rich with no real jobs, or real jobs that they could do badly because their parents owned the companies. Instead, all they did was party and do drugs. I met them out one night while partying with a close friend and her then boyfriend, who was much older and well-connected. He'd introduced us all and for some reason they took a liking to me, so I started to tag along when they went out, like I was a lost puppy they had found on the street and adopted.

On our nights out, nobody really cared how old you were. As long as you were beautiful, rich, or with the beautiful and the rich, the velvet rope parted for you. I had an amazing fake ID, but I was never actually carded. Instead, one of the socialite girls would grab my hand as we approached the sacred doors of whatever club we were attending that night, and the bouncer would pull back the velvet rope in perfect rhythm without us even having to break stride.

We partied like it was a job. There were rituals and timetables and rules of the game. I'd show up in New York and they'd tell me what hot new fancy restaurant to meet them at. Dinner always started at an ungodly late hour, so I'd caffeinate myself not only for the pick-me-up but also to satiate the clawing hunger in my gut. Now, I could kick myself for not tasting so much as a bite at these Michelin-starred restaurants. But at the time, I was an expert at rearranging my plate so that it seemed like I'd actually ingested items on it. The girls always made fun of me for it in a loving way, calling me the little bird. I'd drink at the dinners, though, oh, would I drink.

I can't begin to imagine what these meals cost, between the food and the booze and the clumsily broken plates and stolen silverware. Because, yes, of course the wealthiest of the wealthy are always kleptos. These girls would steal silver, napkins, they'd steal a fucking mirror out of the bathroom if they could get it off the wall and out to a cab. Most strangely of all, we never paid for the meals. Nobody ever paid. As if these girls' presence alone at these hot new spots was payment enough.

I look back on this time in my life like a piece of interactive theater—like I was in *Sleep No More*, and someone was ushering me from room to room, playing out a story for me to watch and learn from. It certainly was entertainment and I certainly did feel like an audience member. But I cannot deny the fact that I was also a part of the act.

After dinner, we would head to Twenty-Seventh Street, and depending on the night we would go to one of three clubs. Most times we ended up at Bungalow 8. The space was small, and the bodies were always crammed in so tightly you had to shove your way through like a salmon swimming upstream. I loved how loud and hot and cramped it was, like being inside of an expensive, debaucherous womb. It felt constrictive and claustrophobic in a way that made me feel safe. Like an elective straitjacket.

I'd drink until I felt fluid, like melted taffy. And then I would dance until I'd sweat out all the alcohol. And then I would start again. The feeling of being on that dance floor, violently jostled by bodies on every side of me, held up by their drunken dancing as I partook in mine, my blood thick with wine and endorphins? That was probably the closest I came to joy as a teenager.

Eventually we'd leave the clubs, piling into cabs, sprawled across each other, windows down no matter what season, yelling into the void of New York City whatever drunken obscenities came to mind, ending up at strangers' apartments where vat-like bowls of cocaine sat in the middle of tables with straws beside them.

This freedom was a drug in and of itself. In New York, with these people, I got to live an alternate reality. One that was free of the crippling social anxiety I felt around my classmates, the concerned eyes of my friends, the questions about my weight, the crushing loneliness and confusion and despair I felt about my future. The fears that I would never make it as an actress, that I would never be skinny enough to love, that I'd never escape the prison of high school, or anorexia, or my own mind. I was unhappy at home. I was lost. And I was afraid. But in New York, I let go, I was released, and all of that fell away. I felt like I was invincible.

I went on like this for a while. Flying back and forth whenever I could convincingly make up a reason to. Falling into their current and letting it take me. It felt good, to live in their world. To give up control and let them dress me and play with me like their doll.

When you party together there is an expedited intimacy that occurs. A connection that knits together more quickly than the one with a friend you go to yoga with or get to know over coffee. Because drunk and drugged, you are your most primal, base selves together, and it makes you feel like you've seen into each other's souls. It isn't real. But it feels like it is. There was one girl in particular I'd gotten closest to. She was sweet in her entitled, bitchy, unimaginably rich kind of way. But at the time, she was the closest thing to a friend I had. I liked her. And she seemed to like me. As someone who wasn't super accustomed to having friends, that was enough for me.

I was back in LA, living my other life as a teenager, when she texted me begging me to come to New York to see her. "I'm bored," she said. "Come visit meeeeee." And so I did. I hopped on a plane and made my way across the country looking forward to a week of forgetting myself within the speed of their fast-paced lives. But when I arrived I found out the rest of the group was away on vacation. It was nearing Christmastime and they had all flown off to the various spots in the world where they spent their winter holidays. This girl wasn't close with her family, though, and had stayed behind. As the holidays are wont to do, they had forced her into a deep depression. I soon realized she hadn't texted me to come have a good time; she had asked me to come to console her. Which I tried my best to do, but honestly, I think she wanted to wallow.

We went out every night, and instead of the carousel of hedonism I was accustomed to with this crowd, there was only a sense of a dark, desperate search for escape. She didn't want to party to enjoy herself. Much like me, she wanted to party simply to escape the ache. I tried to help her keep her chin up, to be a good wingman, a fun-loving companion. But living in the storm of depression myself, I wasn't very good at it.

My last night in the city, we went to Bungalow 8. I had hoped that the magic of the club itself would make for a good night and help cheer us both up. When we arrived, though, the vibe inside the mystical nightclub felt soured, heavy somehow, as if someone had leaked sadness in through the air vents. I lost her in the crowd for hours, which is saying a lot since that club was the size of an airport bathroom. When I finally found her she was slumped on a low couch crying drunkenly into her hands. Her bones held the dull weight of the I-don't-know-how-many-fucking-drinks she had consumed. I weighed about ninety pounds at the time, so trying to hoist her floppy body up off of that low couch was quite the feat. Finally, after what felt like ages, I got her up and headed toward the door, and I was coaxing her with tales of hot chocolate and pajamas when she tripped, forcing me to slightly bump into someone next to me.

I turned around to apologize when a girl twice my size with nails the length of my forearm flipped around to face me.

"Did you just fucking shove me?" she said while pointing one weapons-grade fingernail straight at my eyeball.

"I'm so sorry," I said. "I didn't shove you. My friend is super drunk and she tripped and I bumped into you. I'm so sorry."

"You just fucking shoved me. Baby! Baby! This fucking bitch just fucking shoved me. Are you trying to start something? Baby! This bitch is trying to start something."

It all happened so fast. Obviously I wasn't trying to start anything. I have never wanted to start anything in my life. For better or worse, I am a grade-A pushover. But here was this woman, waving her talons at my face, yelling for her "Baby" somewhere else in the club, and attempting to defend her territory because according to her, I had declared war. Meanwhile, I was trying to apologize and explain while also continuing to hold up my drunken deadweight friend.

At that moment, he emerged from the crowd, walked right past his girlfriend, strode right up to me, and shoved me in the chest.

"You fucking trying to start something with my girl?!"

It was Axl Rose. He looked like shit. He looked strung out, and it looked like he had white powder all over his nose.

He shoved me again.

"I asked you a fucking question! You trying to fucking start something with my girl?!"

I wish I could tell you that I had some fantastic retort here. Or that I shoved him back. Or that I grabbed my friend and ran. But honestly, my brain was on overload and all I did was stand there, like a possum playing dead, holding my friend and our jackets.

He took advantage of my paralysis and grabbed the coats out of my hands. He threw my friend's coat on the ground and then looked at mine. It was a faux-fur vintage coat that I had found in a thrift store in the middle of nowhere, and I loved it. Apparently, so did Axl Rose. He put it on and started rubbing himself all over.

"Oooh, I like this coat! I'm gonna keep this coat. I look fucking good in this coat. This is mine now. Don't you like my coat?!"

He went on and on as he stared daggers straight into my eyes. I truly think if there were fewer witnesses the man would have physically tried to fight me. When he was finally done with his performance, he turned to the two eight-foot-tall bouncers guarding the front door and said, "This girl attacked me. Kick her out and never let her back into this club ever again."

And that was it. They grabbed both of us like we were Beanie Babies and in one fell swoop chucked us out the front door and onto the freezing New York winter streets.

It was pouring rain outside. If it had been two degrees colder, it would have been snowing. I stood there in a total daze trying to process the sequence of events that had just transpired, but it all felt like too much to even begin to compute. I just kept seeing flashes: her nails, his hands on my chest, my coat, the white residue under his nose.

My friend groaned as if she were waking up.

"What happened?" she asked.

I hadn't looked over at her during the debacle, too ensconced in my own survival to worry about anything else. Seemingly, she had drunkenly dozed through the last twenty minutes of insanity.

I turned to her to say something, but as I opened my mouth, nothing came out. What the fuck do you say? Axl Rose just tried to start a fight with me and I think his girlfriend wants to hunt me down and kill me and he stole both our coats and we've been banned from Bungalow 8 forever? Instead I said nothing, stepping onto the curb to try to hail a cab.

My friend whined on the curb. "It's cold. Where's my coat?"

I told her it was gone. I told her that she'd lost it in the club. She started to cry, which was all I wanted to do, sit down on the fucking wet freezing curb and cry. But I knew if I started too I'd never stop. So instead I stood there in the street in the pouring rain, my hand raised high, waiting for the light of the cab to come and take us away from this alternate-universe hell.

All I could think about was Axl Rose sitting mere feet away, behind that huge metal door, within the warmth of the club wearing my coat. At that moment, I knew that it was over. The high had lost its potency and I realized that the flying I'd been experiencing was actually just free-falling and I had finally hit the ground.

I never saw that girl again, or any of that group for that matter. I went to Bungalow 8 a few more times, but it was never the same. The magic was gone. I had a little ways to go yet before hitting rock bottom, but it was close. I could taste it and I knew deep down that recovery was on the horizon. I'd like to think that I would have found my way there on my own, even without the door closing on my *Sliding Doors* New York party existence, but I can't deny that it helped push me there. In a bizarre way I suppose I have to thank Axl Rose for ruining the vibe and releasing me from the spell of that destructive time.

So, thank you, Axl.

But also, can I have my coat back?

YOU SEND ME

In movies when people are about to die and their lives flash before their eyes, it always goes back to the beginning. But I don't think that's how memory works. At least, that's not how my memory works. Maybe that's singular to my brain or maybe it's simply a system malfunction from years of substance abuse and malnourishment and trauma. But when I try to recollect things that have happened to me, my brain rarely takes me back to the beginning. Normally it drops me into the part of the story that left behind the most residue. The dent in the table that snags your fingernail if you run your hand down it. That part of the story, at least for me, is more often than not the most traumatic part. And, I have found, that part almost always takes place at the end.

So that's where we'll begin today. At the end of this particular story.

We pulled into the parking lot of the motel. I stayed in the car as he went inside to secure our room. The shame held me in a bear hug. We'd stayed at this motel once before at the beginning, when we were sick with love. The sign out front reminiscent of the Vegas strip, calling to all those looking for a cave to commit their sins. The flashing lights a beacon to the lost wandering souls, moths to a flame. Come act out your wickedness inside these sad walls. As long as you pay nobody cares, nobody judges, there is no one to answer to other than yourself. Whatever goes on in those rooms washed clean once the bill is settled up.

The room was sobering. Even though I wasn't drunk. It was bleak enough to shock me to attention. There were two bullet holes in the headboard. I traced them with my finger as he fumbled with the lock. Sealing us into this pay-by-the-hour prison. He was drunk to a level I'd never seen before. Which was saying a lot. He'd been a varying degree of intoxicated since I'd met him. But this was something else. The deadness that usually spread over his eyes morphed into something beyond, as if they weren't even inside his skull any longer. As if part of him had disappeared.

The sheets were dirty, filthy, covered in stains I didn't want to know the cause of. He tore them off the bed, revealing an equally stained mattress that he threw me down onto. He'd lost almost all ability to control his motor functions. He ripped my clothes off so aggressively he tore my underwear in half. His hands groped and prodded and grabbed in ways that simply hurt, that made no sense. He didn't even know what part of me he was touching. His monkey brain just wanted sex and I had a hole and we were on a bed.

And I let him.

Because my brain kept telling me, "You love this man. He is your oxygen. He is your reason for living. Every fiber of your being craves him."

Meanwhile, my body told a different story. The usual hunger between my legs that his touch elicited was gone. But he didn't notice as he pinned me down and attempted to thrust his semi-soft dick into the unwelcoming dryness. Thrusting harder and harder until eventually he was inside me. And then he just pounded. My back up against the bed frame, he pounded so hard my entire spine bruised. He pounded so hard that we slid down the sheetless bed onto the dirty carpet. And he kept pounding.

The pain dripped through every pore, but I stopped caring. I think some part of me knew that this scenario, this level of pain, needed to happen to finally get me to understand that I had to get out. So I gave into it. I went limp. And eventually he came and fell asleep.

I lay there for a bit as his dick slowly slid out of me, his cum dripping down my leg. Eventually I wandered into the bathroom. Bathed in the fluorescent lights I stared at myself in the mirror, disgusted by what I saw. My face was smeared in black eyeliner and mascara—things I had put on earlier in the night, wanting to look pretty for him, now covering my face in smudged messy lines. I didn't recognize myself. I hated the person I saw. I hated what she was allowing to happen to her. I wanted to punch my own reflection. To shatter the mirror in front of me.

Instead I took the only towel in the bathroom, a small washcloth the texture of sandpaper, and I scrubbed my face with hot water until all the makeup was gone. I scrubbed so hard with that harsh washcloth that I broke skin on my cheeks and created a rash under my eyes. But I couldn't stop, I couldn't stop scrubbing. I scrubbed for an hour until my face went numb.

A week later he slept with the sister of one of our friends—a gorgeous heroin addict with hep B, which somehow, magically, I didn't get. He'd been sleeping with both of us, unprotected, for months, I found out. That night in the motel was the last time I'd ever see him.

So, you know how it ended.

Now I'll tell you how it began.

-《《◆》》-

For a while, when I was seventeen, I tried on a club kid persona. I hated clubs but attempted to like them because the noise and the late nights and the drinking drowned out, ever so slightly, my depression and loneliness and the eating disorder I didn't want to admit I had. So I partied. I went out religiously. There were certain nights in certain clubs and I was there, every week, like it was my job. In a way it was—chasing something to fill the void while also running from every ounce of feeling that was hunting me like a hungry grizzly bear. If I wasn't going to face my problems I had to flee them, and that was full-time work. My office hours started at 11:00 p.m. and went until it was time to go home.

Some of you are probably wondering, Where were your parents? At the time, I was living with my father, and he was usually home, sleeping soundly. It's not that he didn't care, but for better or worse he trusted me. We had a "don't ask, don't tell" agreement, one that formed organically without discussion. He never gave me a curfew and I never inquired about when I should be home. As long as I came home in one piece, he didn't seem to mind.

If he'd known what I was actually doing, I imagine, he'd have inflicted stricter rules, rules at all. He probably thought I was at some friend's house drinking cheap vodka by a pool and maybe smoking a joint. But he chose blissful ignorance, and so I was able to gallivant to my little rebellious heart's desire. Not that I actually enjoyed it, as I said before. But the partying served a purpose. It numbed the pain, so I took it like medicine.

Every Friday night, my friends and I went to Teddy's at the Roosevelt Hotel. Teddy's was dark and loud and cloudy with cigarette smoke. Filled with the young and the beautiful doing stupid shit and drinking away their feelings and pretending to feel important and have a purpose because they were at the place on the night and the girl who worked the velvet rope had let them in so that must mean they were worth something.

That's where I first saw him. Standing next to the dance floor.

The moment I laid eyes on him, electricity seeped through my veins. At that moment, I fell in love and felt the pain of the inevitable heartbreak—as if my body knew that being with him would be the greatest high I'd ever known, but I would pay the price. I didn't care. I just knew that I had to be with that man.

We were introduced by a mutual friend a few hours after I first saw him. The crowd at Teddy's was winding down, so the party moved, and I moved with it and him. I would have gone to Mars on the back of a dolphin if that's what he was doing.

We ended up at someone's house. I don't even remember how I got there. It didn't matter. What mattered was that we found each other in the kitchen and sequestered ourselves there for hours. I sat on the counter swinging my legs—my best attempt at seeming nonchalant. He leaned on the wall across from me, playing with the cap of his beer. I don't remember what we talked about. But it doesn't matter. That night, we were the only two people who existed in the world.

He was tall with long hair and sad eyes. He was seven years older than me and everything about him—his size, his age, his talent—made me feel small in a way I liked, in a way I needed to feel, like he could cup me in his hands and I could disappear into him.

When the night ended, my friend and I drove him home. He lived in an apartment on the Sunset Strip. I walked him to his front door, and as my friend waited in the car, he asked to kiss me. I had to stand on my tippy-toes to reach my mouth to his.

When we kissed, my body ascended into the clouds.

Two nights later we had our first date. He invited me over, answering the door in a red vintage polo sweater and grinning from ear to ear, his hair brushed to the side. I remember thinking he reminded me of a hot young Mister Rogers.

I had agonized over what to wear. I hated my body. Even though my weight on the scale kept dropping as I continued to starve myself, the hatred in me still grew. So I hid within my clothing. I settled on black skinny jeans, black over-the-knee vintage boots, and an oversized sweater.

We drank red wine out of chipped mugs and talked all night. I

have no memory of anything that was said, because the world was simultaneously void of all senses and exploding around me like Pop
Rocks. Eventually we made our way to what I assumed was his room
but I would later find out was his roommate's. We got under the cov-
ers fully clothed and stared into each other's eyes. We lay there like
that for hours. And finally, after the world had woken up and the room
was bathed in light, he kissed me again. Once more, my physical body
faded, and all that existed was his touch.

Growing up, I was a chubby kid, a dork. Boys and other kids didn't
really like me, and I was bullied horrifically. "Late bloomer" doesn't
even really begin to describe me. So this boy falling for me, this prince
of Los Angeles? It all felt too good to be true. And you know what? It
was. But at the beginning . . . it's what painkillers feel like before the
withdrawal sets in.

Looking back on it now, I can see it coming from miles away. Like
an oasis in the desert with huge blinking neon signs that say, DON'T
STOP HERE! KEEP WALKING OR TURN BACK. WARNING! DANGER! HEART-
BREAK! KEEP AWAY YOU FUCKING IDIOT IT LOOKS NICE BUT THIS PLACE
WILL EVISCERATE YOU IN WAYS YOU DIDN'T KNOW POSSIBLE!!! But at the
time, I was young and naive and insecure. And he was tall and melancholy and a guitar player.

I was a fucking goner.

-《《《◆》》》-

After that first night we were inseparable. We'd go out most nights like
everyone did, meeting his friends at whatever bar or club had been
chosen as the meaningful place to be that evening. I wasn't drinking as
much at the time because I had started eating food again and I didn't

want the extra calories. (I was still in the deep throes of my anorexia, which he didn't notice until months into our relationship, when I felt I should explain to him why we never ate a meal together. Until then, he'd never asked.) But he'd drink enough for the both of us.

I don't remember specifics about those evenings. I suppose I've blocked them out a bit or my then-malnourished brain didn't retain them in full. I see snippets, though: Beautiful people milling about in dark bars, drinking and smoking cigarettes. All the right music being played for people to either dance to or not dance at all. We always stayed out late, so very late.

I do remember constantly being tired during that period of my life. Exhausted. A type of to-your-bones exhaustion where just the sheer act of keeping your eyes open and your mind alert enough to listen feels impossible. But he wanted to go out, so out we went.

I still couldn't believe that he wanted me. And every time we stepped out into the world, his world, surrounded by his friends and his environment, the effortlessly hip and intelligent and erudite darlings of the LA youth, I never felt like I belonged. I always felt like an outsider, someone they would never accept, someone they thought didn't deserve him. But I always went, to be with him, always suited up in the same vintage leather jacket, like armor.

Those nights, he'd hold my hand and kiss me and whisper into my ear how beautiful I was. And when it was finally time to go home we'd get into his car and all those beautiful important people who thought I wasn't good enough for him wouldn't matter anymore. Because he was mine.

Driving home, always late. Or was it early? We'd always debate at what point time switches from late to early. 2:00 a.m.? 3:00 a.m.? Never?

On those drives, the world belonged to us. The only two awake and alive to breathe in the energy of the night. As we drove, windows down, the usually traffic-jammed Los Angeles highways were empty. The sweet California night breeze filled the car. At the right time of year, the smell of jasmine engulfed us—a scent you almost can't believe is real, it's so honeyed and thick. When the jasmine hit I'd breathe even deeper, inhaling it like candied oxygen.

I was so in love, so sickly in love.

I'd lay my head in his lap as he drove. His blue 1980s Volvo trustily cruising along, despite how wasted he was. We'd play Elvis radio and it felt like nothing in the world could be wrong or out of place, like we could stay there always, never having to leave or grow old or be sad, a fissure in time that we could hide away in, forever in love, forever happy, the King singing us to sleep.

At his place, we slept on the pullout couch in the living room, having been relegated there because his brother, with whom he shared a room, wouldn't let us use the bedroom, convinced all we'd do was fuck.

One night, a few months in, after fucking on that romantic sleeper sofa, my back still sore from the center bar digging deeply into my anorexic frame, he took me by the hand and led me over to their record player.

It was the prized possession of the household, the most expensive thing they owned. I'd say it probably cost more than a few months of their rent. It was sandwiched on either side by two huge speakers and a pair of studio-grade headphones in case you didn't want to share your listening experience.

Music was sacred to him and his brother, something to be worshipped, each record in their collection like a chapter of scripture. People who didn't fully understand or appreciate it were heathens, unworthy, going to a plebeian hell where French New Wave movies and Norman Mailer novels and deep cuts didn't exist, a place where top 40 played on repeat.

Using that record player, he taught me about music. He taught me about T. Rex and the Kinks, and B-sides. He inducted me into the church of brilliantly orchestrated sound and he taught me why and how to worship it.

That night, he sat me down and put those giant headphones over my ears. So gently, like I was something that might break. The house was dark and everyone else was asleep. There was a full moon and I could see it out of his living room window, the only light around us coming off that full spotlight in the sky. I stared at it as I waited for his next move.

He gingerly slipped an album from its sleeve and placed it on the record player, handling it like it was a precious jewel, finding the exact groove he was looking for. (He knew the geography of each record like the back of his hand. I always imagined he could see the notes within each one of those plain black grooves.) The needle dropped. And then "You Send Me" by Sam Cooke melted into my ears. He stared at me and held my hand. And I stared back.

The song ended and that crinkle at the end of the record took over. White noise washing over my numb body. He took the headphones off me and said, "I love you." And everything went quiet and the void that had always existed within me disappeared. Filled by his love.

At this point in my memory I no longer see the moon.

—≪≪◆≫≫—

For a while, things were good.

He didn't have a job when we met. An out-of-work guitar player.

But eventually he landed a job at A.P.C. He was good at it, he fit the part, he fit the clothes. And he loved it because, A.P.C. being a French company, he could drink on his lunch hour.

The sex wasn't great—I never had an orgasm while we were to-gether. I don't think he ever asked, or even noticed, whether or not I was enjoying it. But I didn't care. He was touching me, he was inside me, I had him. And for the time being, that satiated me in the pleasure department. Or at least I thought it did.

When people were around and the pullout couch was being used as a couch, we'd have sex in the bathroom at his apartment. The ceiling was barely high enough to fit his six-foot-four frame. The sink was caked in years of toothpaste sediment and beard trimmings and grime. The ceiling above the shower infested with mold so thick it looked like wallpaper. The toilet . . . well, I'll let you use your imagination there. He'd lay a towel down on the never-cleaned bathroom floor and lay me down on top of it and fuck me until he came, my head banging up against the door frame and my right knee often getting burned on the wall heater placed in the perfectly inconvenient spot.

You know how they say love is blind? When you're young, it's blind and fucking idiotic. I loved him so deeply I couldn't see how un-happy I was. It's like those stories you hear of people who are so high, they accidentally put their hand on a scalding hot pan and burn all their skin off without realizing it because they're too numb to clock the pain. When you're that high, you don't care because the drugs are surging through your veins and that's all you feel—the synthetic joy. That was me. My hand was sitting directly on the burner, my skin melting, a lovesick smile plastered on my face. Totally oblivious to the damage being done.

The beginning of that year was a euphoric blur.

When we were together, I'd dream of us lying in bed. And as I looked down I'd see that I was pregnant, very pregnant, and he was stroking my bursting belly and staring at me with the purest of joy in his eyes. I'd wake from those dreams feeling satiated, full, complete. I saw our future so clearly, so convinced he would be the only love I'd ever know.

We used to drive up the windy hill behind his apartment. The road snaked dangerously up and up and up toward the California sky. The neighborhood was filled with homes. Not just houses, or at least not to us, but homes. We would daydream about our future home and even picked one out. Driving up, it was on the left side of the road, right at a bend. A small ranch house with a little front yard. We would have a bulldog and there would always be a record playing. And the house would forever be filled with love and music and something baking in the oven. It was a nice dream.

Eventually the reality of his addiction started to break through the hard sugar coating we had encased ourselves in.

Addicts are charming and talkative and ever so clever at the art of distraction. Sleight-of-hand artists, if you will. Look over here at me being the perfect boyfriend! Look, look, watch my hands as I make magic and awe you with my tricks. But while they're distracting you with that, they're actually slowly eroding your sense of self-worth and your definition of love. As the snake charm wears off, you realize you have fallen for someone who is killing themselves one whiskey sour at a time.

The realization that I was dating an addict happened slowly. Probably because I didn't want to believe it. And probably because addicts are so good at hiding their addictions. But when I couldn't ignore it any longer, it felt like it was too late to turn back. I was eighteen, I was in love for the first time. I could fix him. I could make him better.

He always drank, but in the beginning I never noticed how much.

Everyone drank. We were surrounded by young, hot socialite crea-
tures. Pretty much the only time they weren't holding a cocktail in
one hand and a cigarette in the other was when they were asleep. So I
never clocked his level of alcohol consumption. And he was good at
hiding his level of inebriation. Most drunks are. They can be well over
the legal limit and you'd never even know they're buzzed. But the
longer we were together, the more I began to notice just how much
alcohol he consumed, and that he never stopped. I'd watch him drink,
at parties, bars, dinners. If there was alcohol of any kind in front of
him or readily available, he'd ingest it. And once the glass was empty
he'd just keep filling it, ordering more. I don't think he realized how
much he was drinking. Once he started, he couldn't stop until he
blacked out or fell asleep or the alcohol was gone.

His eyes were the thing that finally tipped me off. Those gorgeous
eyes that I loved so much, that I would stare stupidly into for hours,
they became something else when he was drunk. They'd go black.
The man I loved disappearing into an inebriated dark hole, replaced
by a dumb sloppy stranger.

Dead eyes. That's what I came to call him.

Alcoholics never think they're drunk or as drunk as they are. So
most of our arguments centered around that. But I always knew when
he'd crossed the danger threshold because I'd be talking to him and all
of a sudden he'd be gone. Instead of my human boyfriend standing in
front of me, there'd just be a meat suit with dead fish eyes looking
through me as I talked.

"You're drunk," I'd say.

He always denied it. Not once did he ever own up to his true level
of inebriation. To this day I don't fully understand why. Was it stub-
bornness? Pride? Did he truly not understand how drunk he was?

Our biggest fights centered around driving. When his eyes went dead and I knew he was no longer coherent, I'd ask to drive home. This always led to screaming matches. He'd swear he wasn't drunk. I'd cite the twenty-plus beers, cocktails, shots he'd consumed. He'd be incensed I accused him of being too drunk to drive. He'd tell me that he'd never put me in that kind of danger. He'd accuse me of not trusting him, of being a bad partner, of not loving him enough. He'd call me names, he'd scream obscenities.

These fights happened in almost every bar parking lot in Los Angeles, always escalating to me attempting to grapple the keys from his hands. But he had a full foot on me, and my five-foot-four, one-hundred-pound body wasn't really a match for anyone. Not to mention, drunken anger can make people do crazy things. He wasn't a super fit guy, but when he was drunk and wanted something, he became freakishly strong.

Eventually I'd give in. He'd drive us home. Always safely too. Never once did we get into an accident, get pulled over, or even so much as swerve.

Why the fuck did you get in the car with him?! That's what you're thinking, right? I've asked myself this question so many times. And the answer? I don't know. But the even weirder thing? I was never scared. I should have been, but I wasn't. I think I loved him too much.

Anyone who has loved an addict knows that they make it nearly impossible for you to climb out of their web. Every time they break a promise or your heart or relapse, they are just convincing enough to make you believe that really, for sure, no questions asked, this was the last time.

It never is.

Every Wednesday night we'd go to the same Mexican restaurant with his best friend and his best friend's girlfriend. Our standing double date. We didn't go there for the food or the ambience. We went because every Wednesday they had five-dollar margaritas that came in goblets. He would drink a minimum of five of them.

One night he drank ten.

He could barely walk to the car. After another fight about letting me drive home, I got into the passenger seat and something inside me broke. I told him he had to choose. That it was either me or alcohol.

Without so much as a fight he told me he'd give it up. That he wanted to marry me. That he loved me more than anything in the world. He sobbed and begged for forgiveness and admitted to knowing and seeing the depth of his addiction and the damage it was causing. He promised he'd change, that he'd do anything to keep me. He swore on our love that he would never have another drink again as long as he lived.

I believed him. I think he believed himself too.

-«‹‹◆››»-

He stayed sober for a week.

Seven days later, we went back to that Mexican restaurant for our standing double date. We sat down, and the sweet waitress, oblivious to our troubles, came over and innocently asked what she could get us all to drink. Without skipping a beat he ordered two margaritas.

I stared into the chip bowl for the entire dinner and didn't say a single word. And on the car ride home when he asked me what was wrong, I calmly asked him if margaritas were considered alcohol or if I had somehow missed something.

He said, "What, did you expect me to not have a margarita on margarita night?"

I felt like an airplane whose emergency door had suddenly flown off midflight, the freezing cold winds of thirty thousand feet interrupting the calm recycled air. I had been thrust into the bright, cold, loud world of reality and there was no going back.

That night, as he drove down Sunset Boulevard, I realized I was dating a very serious alcoholic who, yes, maybe couldn't help himself, but he also couldn't love me because of that. And unless I left, I was going to be collateral damage for the rest of my life.

Somehow, somewhere in the depths of my lovesick cripplingly insecure mind, I found the wherewithal to end it that night in his apartment. We both sobbed so hard our noses stopped working and screamed so much our voices gave out.

I drove home alone in the wee hours of the morning feeling numb but also weightless and free. Terrified for the pain awaiting me once the adrenaline wore off but also like I had just avoided a death sentence.

But addicts don't let you off that easy . . .

Hours later, at 6:00 a.m., he drove to my house. My family was out of town and I was alone, which he knew. He stood outside my window on the roof of his car screaming my name.

I didn't break up with him because I wanted to. I had done it because some smarter part of my brain knew I should. But when it comes to matters of the heart, desire is much more powerful than intelligence.

I let him in.

He begged for my forgiveness. He sobbed and groveled and lay at my feet, clawing at my legs, promising me anything, everything, things he had and things he didn't. I told him I couldn't trust him anymore. He swore to me he'd change. He'd stop drinking for real this time. He'd never touch another drop until the day he died. I told him I didn't believe him, that he'd said that before. He said he'd do anything if I took him back. I told him I couldn't. And then we had sex.

Because I lost the strength to fight against what I actually wanted: to believe him.

After, I lay in his arms as the sun came up knowing that I was wrong and weak and only prolonging my own pain. But I couldn't help myself.

That morning, lying naked in bed, we made a pact. We wouldn't "officially" be together. We'd still "break up," but we'd keep going as usual. In order to rationalize it we made rules: No kissing in public or in front of friends. We'd tell everyone we'd broken up (they all knew this was bullshit). And we'd still stay monogamous even though we weren't technically together. If one of us ever wanted out of the arrangement or found someone else, we had to tell the other one before acting on anything. In essence we were in an open relationship. A deeply dysfunctional, codependent open relationship that wasn't actually open because we were still unhealthily in love with each other.

Looking back now, this plan reminds me of some horrible, unfinanced indie script I'd read and pass on even when I desperately needed a job because it had so many holes and the plot didn't add up. Also the ending fucking sucked, and you could guess what it was from page one.

But in my not-fully-formed eighteen-year-old brain, it made perfect sense at the time.

We did this for another year.

He kept on drinking. Doubled down on it, actually. He was like a wounded animal in an open field—reclusive and sharp around the edges, skittish and cruel and always hunting for a fight. He started drinking at work. He almost lost his job, he could barely pay his rent. His car kept getting impounded. His friends in a hugely successful band offered him a gig as a guitarist on their world tour, and he turned it down for no good reason. I watched as he ruined his life and squandered his talent, and I was helpless to stop it. And the more he drank, the more self-destructive he became, and the more resentful I became. The anger and sadness building inside me began to calcify, turning into something hard and unfeeling. I was alive—I was breathing and existing and waking up and going to sleep—but it was all just rote action. I was empty.

-≪≪◆≫≫-

He joined me the night my stepmother threw a massive blowout at our house for my father's sixtieth birthday. There were hundreds of people there, family, friends, many of whom I had known since I was born, many of whom had employed me, or I hoped one day might.

He got so wasted he could barely stand. And then he tried to have sex with me in my bedroom, which that night was doubling as the coat closet. It was at the base of the stairs and just to the left of the front door and very much within earshot of the party happening just outside. He sloppily shoved me in there and began aggressively trying to strip me naked. I protested, but he continued to grope. And finally, I think possibly in an attempt to be romantic, he lifted me up off my feet into his arms. But being more whiskey than he was water at the time, he lost his grip and dropped me on the floor. From six foot four, that's quite a long way down. Half the party rushed in to see what the loud thump was, and there we were. Me half naked, tangled on the floor crying. Him with his pants around his ankles drunk beyond comprehension.

And that was it. Well, I told myself it was. Even though we kept trucking along just as we were. But I told myself I needed to officially pull the plug. That I couldn't see him any longer. That this had to stop.

The following week he took me to the motel.

Which brings us back to where we began.

—《《◆》》—

I wish you could be hospitalized for heartbreak. I imagine it like a kind of appendicitis—something inside your body is exploding within itself, infecting and destroying every ounce of you from within. You implode by exploding.

Although maybe that's not right. Heartbreak isn't an explosion. It's more precise, more painful, more pointed than that. It isn't messy, it's malicious. It is a shattering. Like a glass bottle being hit with a bullet and bursting into pieces too numbered to count. That's what happens within your chest. Your heart fragmenting into tiny shards that scatter within you, slicing open everything they come in contact with.

You know you'll never be well again. You'll never smile again. Laughing is off the table entirely because you've forgotten how to do it. Eating and drinking are no longer essential and sleep is something you either would sell both your kidneys for, but even then it won't come, or it's the only thing you're capable of doing and the thought of leaving your bed leaves you even more comatose than you already were. The tears come in floods, and when they dry up, the dry heaving begins.

When you do venture out into the world, all you feel is hatred and confusion at the people walking down the street like everything is fine. Because everything IS NOT FUCKING FINE. Everything is broken, irreparably. How can they not see that? How can they smile and hold hands and buy groceries like life is just going as usual? Can't they see that the earth has been thrown off its axis and that you basically swallowed glass and you are no longer a human but just a skin outline filled with pain?

The pain is so heavy. Honestly, you wish for appendicitis, you wish for a horrific car accident or a cancer diagnosis or to be attacked by a rabid coyote. You wish for something that would put the pain on the outside, show the significance of it, the level of hurt, the damage that has been done. You want people to see it. But they can't because it's hidden deep within you.

If only it had been appendicitis instead.

When you have your heart broken, you think you're the only one who has ever felt that specific color of hurt, that nobody else would or could understand the level of pain you're experiencing. And you're certain that it will never pass, that you will never feel well again, that you will never be happy, that this heartache will never subside.

But it does, eventually.

My heart stayed shattered within my chest for a long time, until eventually, I met someone new, someone who started to help put the broken parts of me back together.

But even today I wonder if there aren't still a few pieces of glass floating around somewhere in my body. Perhaps that's what happens to everyone when they have their heart broken. Maybe there's always a little piece that stays cracked. A reminder, a memory of the pain that teaches you not to repeat it, one that makes the true love you eventually find that much more rewarding.

Because as Leonard Cohen said, the cracks are where the light comes in.

100 LBS.

I wanted to be 100 pounds.

I knew once I got there everything would be okay. I knew it in the depths of my soul, trusted that by the time I arrived at the safe harbor of a certain number on a scale I would be okay. I was determined if nothing else. I just wanted to weigh 100 pounds.

I had tried for so long, too long, to secure the bigger, deeper, more primal things I so desired. It wasn't working. I thought I must be doing it wrong. So I changed tactics and adopted one that I thought would get me there faster. I started to starve myself. And it worked. It worked really fucking well, actually . . . for a while.

I was damn good at it too. I aced it. Which came with its own form of satisfaction. A job well done. And the smaller I got the safer I felt. But the safety was only temporary, fleeting. I'd stand on solid ground for a time until suddenly the floor below me would morph and liquify. Concrete to hot lava in minutes, seconds. And I would have to move, run, find solid ground again to save myself. I'd have to be smaller, skinnier, LESS in order to be safe again.

One hundred seemed like such a good solid number, such a reasonable and realistic number, such a beautiful and perfect number. I could stop trying then because there I would finally be safe. I'd have to maintain there, but that would be easy after the fight I'd gone through to get there. Maintaining is easier than dropping.

I remember the day that number, that magical number came up on the scale. ONE HUNDRED. I stared at it for a long, long time. Breathing it in, waiting for the tidal wave of sunshine and relief to wash through my veins. But nothing happened. It was a dud firework limp in my hand—no explosion, no relief, nothing. My magical potion had not worked. Or I had somehow failed. Maybe my calculations were off. Or the scale was wrong. Or the day, or the weather. Something wasn't right.

So I kept trying. I kept trekking toward my Nirvana knowing that once I finally got there I would feel safe, I would feel loved, I would finally be able to rest. I was so fucking tired all the time. Even though I slept as much as I could to avoid the gnawing hunger that melted my brain, I was still so fucking tired. I wanted to rest, I wanted to let go and just stop trying but I knew I couldn't, not until I got there. So I kept going.

The next day I stepped onto the scale, every morning a fresh day of reckoning. Ninety-nine. NINETY-NINE. Ninety-nine pounds and zero ounces. Five foot four and ninety-nine pounds of bones and flesh and fat and dehydration and sadness.

I stared at the number and felt nothing yet again. Keep going, the voice in my head said. The one that talks incessantly and always knows better and always thinks I'm wrong. The one that forces me to open and close the refrigerator at 3:00 a.m. as I fight with it. So hungry I feel I might start pulling off my finger nails just to feel something else. Anything other than hunger. NO! it says. CLOSE THE DOOR, YOU FAT LOSER. WHAT ARE YOU GONNA DO, EAT SOMETHING AND THEN LISTEN TO THE CELLULITE GROW UNDERNEATH YOUR SKIN? GO AHEAD, EAT SOMETHING AND GET FAT AND SEE IF ANYBODY LOVES YOU THEN. So I listen, and I shut the door, but then the hunger, that primal sensation lurking, living, listless in the pit of my stomach drilling a hole into the base of my brain, screams and forces my arms to act, wrenching open the refrigerator. And again the voice speaks. NO NO NO NO NO!! I SAID. FUCKING. NO!!! FAT FAT FAT FAT FAT YOU'RE GONNA GET FAT CLOSE THE FUCKING FRIDGE! And back and forth and back and forth.

I stand in a pitch-black kitchen opening and closing the fridge. The fluorescent bulb basking me in its harsh white light until my anxiety slams the door and I am cast into darkness again.

I continue to weigh myself, every morning, like clockwork. One could call it a ritual. I have started my own little religion worshipping at the shrine of 100 pounds. And the number continues to go down. And all I want is to weigh 100 pounds. Still, that's all I want, all I need, what I MUST have.

98—If only I weighed 100 pounds.

93—If only I weighed 100 pounds.

89—if only I weighed 100 pounds.

88—EIGHTY-EIGHT POUNDS.

This is the lowest I ever got. I don't think I would have minded dying. I wasn't afraid of death. I noticed something during this period: Death is only scary when it's far away. We fear things we cannot comprehend. But once you near it, once you can taste the salt in the ocean air coming off its shores, it is no longer unknown and therefore no longer fearful. Or at least, not in the same way. I didn't want to die but I also just didn't really care. It was close enough that I could smell it, hear it. And it sounded quiet, it sounded calm. I knew if I died, I could stop trying. Like the velvety slip of falling under the water in a bathtub, it is easy and graceful and suddenly sound has lost its power. You are left in peace, floating with only a muffled humming far, far away. That sounded nice to me.

I was so tired.

I don't really recollect my life at this stage. What I did with my days, how I felt, who I loved, what I thought about, I don't remember. Did I contemplate my future? My body could go through the motions of life, of being awake, of being a human, but I couldn't take anything in. I see photographs of myself then and I wonder what I was thinking. I want to hug my past self and cry and scream and comfort life into her, tell her she doesn't want to die, tell her . . . tell her she is loved.

Eighty-eight pounds. The doctors told me that if I dropped any more weight my heart could stop, that I could die. If I kept trying I would try myself to death. They told me my bones were so brittle that they were worse than their ninety-year-old patients. That with the slightest slip I could shatter my pelvis, my back, my ribs—any bone in my body was up for grabs to be ground to dust. I was anemic, I had arthritis, asthma, severe insomnia. I wouldn't sleep for days on end. I couldn't shit, my skin was a minefield of pimples and dark circles. I couldn't focus, couldn't form thoughts or hold conversations or walk up stairs. I felt nothing, I felt numb.

I understood the things they said but they didn't register. I didn't not care, but I definitely didn't care. I coasted. I let life happen to me, go by me. My body was slowly shutting down, powering off. I was walking through my house at the end of the night shutting off lights one by one as I made my way to bed. There weren't many lights left, perhaps the hallway and my bedside lamp. I didn't care, I just wanted to weigh 100 pounds because I knew, if only the doctors could understand what I knew, that once I weighed 100 pounds everything would be okay and they could all stop worrying.

I was a walking manifestation of dysfunction, poised at any moment to trip and shatter, a delicate mess. Handle with care they told me.

I didn't.

I went to New York City for a week to party. I didn't eat, I couldn't eat, couldn't bring myself to. Instead I drank champagne. Not water, never water, just champagne. I danced until I sweat through my clothes. And I walked in the freezing cold midwinter without a proper coat in tiny dresses, if you could even call them that. Dresses so short and flimsy they were basically half a tissue.

One night I came home and I got into bed and I looked out the window of the disgusting friend of a friend of a friend's apartment I was staying in and I saw the moon. And then my heart started to stop. I could feel the beats slowing and slowing and slowing and I knew it was shutting down for good. The fire had gone out and I was ready to turn off my bedside lamp. I wondered if anyone would care and I stared at that moon and asked if it would keep me company while I died. And it did.

I stared at that moon for as long as I can remember as I felt my heart slowly stop beating.

The next morning I woke up. And I continued on just as I had been. For a while.

And then somewhere, somehow, I got back to 100.

Then I passed it.

Somewhere, somehow, I began to emerge from the hole in the ground that I had dug for myself. Somewhere, somehow I decided I didn't want to die. I'm not sure exactly what the moment was but it occurred and that is why I'm not writing this from the great beyond. (Although that would be impressive.)

I still pine for 100 pounds occasionally: the sign of acceptance and forgiveness and unconditional love, things we deserve from the moment we emerge from our mother till the day we flatline and the expanse in between. Things we deserve for the time we are here without question and without requirements. Things that in my mis-wired brain I think I will only get if I am skinny. And yes, I still want 100 pounds, because in my mind, it is safety.

And yet when I lived in the fog of my desire for this golden weight I was anything but safe. I was dancing with death and getting date-raped and drinking to excess and popping pills like Tic Tacs and exposing myself to all different kinds of delicious abuse just to feel something. I let sex be something that happened to me instead of something I chose. I picked friends I didn't even know or like. I stopped being able to taste or cry or sweat. I just stopped.

I often wonder if I would be different if this hadn't been my life for that period of time. Would I? Be different? I don't know. Do I wish I was? Different? Constantly, incessantly, tirelessly yes.

Do I still wish I weighed 100 pounds?

Yes. Often.

The shame is like a hard slap to the face, that sting. Or the numb raw tingling burning of walking through single digit weather for too long. It is harsh and severe and nauseating.

Perhaps not 100 pounds, but less than I am, smaller, thinner, NOT AS BIG. NOT AS MUCH.

Recovery is never ending. There is no 100 pounds in recovery. The road never stops, not until you drop dead and can no longer think or feel or speak and therefore no longer act out, act on, create, or be a part of your dysfunction. Until then it lives inside of you and every day you have to choose to fight it or give into its sweet, delicious tempting talk.

Don't eat that. Just drop a few pounds. You should work out again today. You're not hungry you're just bored. You look obese in that photograph, what are you gonna do about it? You didn't get that job because you're fat. He doesn't love you because you're fat. If you were skinnier you'd be okay. Just lose five pounds, ten pounds, fifteen.

Maybe cut out sugar, fruit, protein, meals, food all together. If you were more disciplined you'd be skinnier. You'd be happier, you'd be more loved. Just stop eating, you did it once before. Just get to 100 pounds.

The voice is there incessantly. It never stops. It's a sneaky mother-fucker and it preys on you when you're down or tired or anxious or waiting at a stoplight.

But here's the thing. What would happen if I just pressed mute? What would happen if I just turned off the voice? What would happen if I erased 100 pounds from my mind and just woke up and lived my life and chose to breathe in through my nose and out through my mouth and step and step and step and look up instead of down?

A friend of mine once said that the living, waking world is where we are for a temporary moment. He described it as if being "alive" is like going to work. We are here at work, this is our office. We are here to learn and work and that's it. At the end of the day when we punch out at 5:00 p.m. and grab our lunch pail and our thermos and head back home, we are done here. And we cross back over to the other side where our family and friends and all of our pets stand waiting for us with open arms, and that is what we call home.

Here is just a job.

But we bring what we learn back.

I wonder what I have to bring back home when I'm done here. I wonder what I've learned, why this happened, why I chose this path. What wisdom did this dysfunction stitch into me that I can impart? I wonder if I'll be happy on the other side. I wonder if I'll be free. I wonder if I feel safe on the other side.

I wonder how much I'll weigh.

Part 2

⟶⟨⟨⟨◆⟩⟩⟩⟶

The Graveyard Shift

PER OUR PREVIOUS
CONVERSATION

When I was a kid, my mother used to take me to the theater with her when she had rehearsal. I loved it there. I crawled around on the floor scrunching myself between seats, hunting for goodies like old gum and candy wrappers and interestingly colored dust bunnies. I'd spend what felt like hours (to my toddler brain at least) worming my way through the floor of the audience pit collecting my treasures in a disposable bowl. Once I had what felt like sufficient "protein," I'd make my way to the greenroom where I'd pull from the fridge any kind of liquid available to my short-armed reach. Then I'd mix it all together with a plastic spoon. I called it Spoolabosh Soup. After, I'd go around to everyone in the theater and asked them to try it. They mimed taking massive bites and loving my creation. I was always completely and utterly content.

I went to sets with my parents too—I loved them as well. I loved the sounds and the smells. I loved the dark corners and all of the wires snaking across the concrete floors. I loved the sense of communal commitment to magic, like everyone was in on the same secret, speaking in hushed tones, aware that we were gaming the system, taking a shortcut, creating something that we would trick people into believing was real but all the while we alone knew the mechanism behind the con.

I have a vivid memory of sitting in my mother's lap as she sat in the chair of the makeup trailer having her hair done. Facing toward the mirror, I imagined a day when it was me sitting in that chair having my hair done, getting ready for a day at work. I don't say this from a place of entitlement, like I knew that this would be available to me as a career, but rather that my family was a part of the circus and I knew in my soul that one day I wanted to be too. That this would be the one place I would fit in.

I understood from an early age that I had to be quiet on set, which I did happily because it meant I was part of the team. I would fit myself into a corner or under a chair or next to an apple box and close my eyes and inhale that smell of a scrim lazily melting under the heat of the light it was married to. I loved the dust and hair spray and face powder and quiet feet and held breath after "ACTION"—the entire protective bubble of those impenetrable soundstage walls holding in our secret world.

I remember visiting set one day when my mother was shooting a birthday scene. Her on-screen son was being served a big, beautiful birthday cake. And in the scene the cake came out, they sang "Happy Birthday," the cake was served, and then they were all supposed to eat it ravenously. And so they did, over and over and over again. I learned about angles that day. How you had to shoot from one direction, then another, then the reverse, then closer. And I remember I was rabid with jealousy that that kid's job that day was to eat cake that many times. I just kept thinking, I want to do that. I WILL do that. One day, that will be me. (Sadly, the reality of a food scene after the age of five is normally stomachache inducing and not as exciting.) But to my five-year-old brain it seemed like heaven.

Cut to twenty years later when I'm sitting in Cafe Mogador at six in the morning on the set of *Girls*. I'm surrounded by Middle Eastern food, and I'm meant to be hungover and ravenous. But in real life, I haven't even had my coffee yet, and all I want is to go back to bed. Instead, the director, Richard Shepard, is telling us that we have to sell that we're trying to soak up the remnants of the alcohol still coursing through our veins with the mounds of hummus and pita sitting in front of us. But the thought of shoving tzatziki in my mouth makes me want to hurl. It's too early, I'm too tired, and I know in terms of camera setups I have at least a wide, the reverse wide, and a couple of sizes on my coverage's worth of food to eat. I try to fake it, but Richard isn't buying it, so I spend the next six hours shoving hummus-soaked pita in my mouth.

By nightfall, I am the beige version of *Willy Wonka*'s Violet Beauregarde, and I think I'll never so much as look at hummus again. Not quite as magical as the day that boy ate cake for hours. But I love my job just as much as I thought I would that day, watching him gorge himself on sugar take after take. Because even though I have chickpeas up to my eyeballs and I am anticipating being constipated for a week, I still somehow, against all odds, have managed to fulfill my dream of running away to join the circus.

My trajectory was always clear to me. And until my friends went to college and all dissolved into existential crises about how the fuck they were meant to decide what they wanted to do with the rest of their lives at the age of eighteen, I never quite realized how lucky I was to have known all along. But I did. And before I graduated high school I had finagled myself an agent. Well, kind of.

I have no illusions about the fact that I started off with a leg up. My entire family is in the industry, back to my grandparents on both sides. I had exposure and I had connections. But the catch is, you still have to be good, because the industry doesn't care how you got yourself an agent, they don't care who your father is; if you biff the audition, you aren't getting the part. Because my parents were in the industry, there was a weird feeling that nobody wanted to go easy on me, like they felt I was already at an advantage, so instead, they went extra hard on me. A leg up will only get you so far—you still have to know how to ride the fucking horse.

My father's agent was a family friend. We'd go to dinners at his overly modern house tucked away in the canyon. He'd throw parties where famous people would mingle comfortably, knowing they were among their own kind. I'd just watch and listen and try to learn. I loved being the youngest person at those parties; it made me feel special, a feeling I rarely had in my daily life. At school, around my peers, I felt like a gum wrapper forgotten at the bottom of someone's coat pocket. But at these parties I was Cinderella right as she entered the ball, at the top of the stairs. It was as if my father had brought a small dog to the party. Everyone wanted to pet me and ask how old I was. Looking back, I realize I wasn't special—I was just an anomaly, i.e., one of these things is not like the other. But either way it felt good at the time.

And I was safe with my father. Even when men, a vast mixture of washed-up nineties leading men or current titans of the industry, would hit on me, I still never felt exposed—I would just return to my dad, like I held a get-out-of-jail-free card. It did always seem odd to me that even when they knew or simply found out that I was my father's daughter, that he was in the other room if I needed to scream for him, that I was underage, they were never deterred. I suppose fame truly does dull your mind to the reality of consequences.

At one party a very famous, very married, much older man kept testing the waters by standing next to me and running his hand lower and lower and lower down the back of my body. I think he thought it was a game. Like chess. I'd move two squares to the left and he'd counter by moving three.

At another party I was waiting for my father's car from the valet while he finished up doing some business inside. An eighties actor attempting a comeback after his umpteenth round of getting clean waited next to me. His expensive vehicle pulled up and the valet handed him the keys. The actor asked my name and if I wanted to go home with him. I told him my name and that my father was inside and I had to wait for him. He asked again if I wanted to go home with him. I told him how old I was. He asked a third time. I said no. And as he walked to his car he threw back, "Okay, your loss."

At a smaller, intimate dinner for my father's agent's birthday, I sat next to a junior agent. He had been my father's agent's assistant for years but had recently been promoted. And my dad, never one to beat around the bush, yelled at this new junior agent across the table and told him he should represent me. With the eyes of my father and my father's agent, his boss, bearing down on him, he didn't really have any available options but to say yes. So that, my friends, is how I got my first agent.

How lucky, you say, how unfair, what an advantage over all those who work so hard and never even get representation. And yes, you would be right. However, I will say there are a few things you need in addition to simply "having" an agent in order for it to mean anything. They need to actually be good at their job, they need to send you on auditions, and they need to like you. Sadly, mine was not the first, occasionally accomplished the second, and in reference to the third, I think he hated me. In his defense, I was forced upon him.

After this dinner I was called into the office of the agency to meet with the junior agent, my father's agent, and a few other men who would be added to "my team" to round it out. I felt like a million bucks. And I left that meeting on cloud nine. Agents always talk a big game, they always promise the world, they always tell you this is what we're gonna do and we'll be off to the races. You leave the meetings feeling like you've already booked a career-breaking role and you're simply waiting for your Emmy nomination to arrive in the mail.

Eventually reality sets in and you realize it was all simply talk. But I still felt grateful. I had agents and that was a lot more than other seventeen-year-old actresses could say. And so the hustle began. They'd send me out on auditions here or there, and then I'd never hear anything. When I called the agents back, they were always busy, on the other line, away from their desks. Sometimes they'd return my phone calls weeks later, and if I missed their call I knew that even if I called back immediately it would be another three weeks before I would hear their voices in real time.

I took to sending handwritten thank-you notes to casting directors, directors, and producers who were in my auditions. I bought myself personalized stationery I couldn't afford because I thought it would look more professional. I would drive to my agency, pay too much money to park in their garage, which was the only parking area for miles around, and drop the handwritten letters in the mailroom so they could be sent out by the agency to the respective recipients. I spoke to the guys in the mailroom more than I spoke to my actual agents. And we liked each other more, developing what I'd go so far as to call a friendship.

I began scouring Actors Access—a resource for casting directors, producers, and agents to know about the current projects and auditions happening. It isn't technically for actors, but a family friend who was a casting director let me use her login, and I'd spend hours each day scanning the site looking for projects and parts I thought I'd be right for. And then I'd send them to my agents asking if they'd submitted me. And they'd never respond directly. But often, a few days later, I'd get an email from them with the projects I had originally suggested, with them saying, "We found this project for you. Take a look and let us know if you're interested and we'll set up an audition." I never called them on it. What good would it do me?

I knew my agents didn't like me very much. It was like dating someone who refused to actually say we were dating but wanted to keep me around, and who was always telling me the things he thought were wrong with me. After I'd send in a tape, the team would call me and say things like, "Did you do your hair differently this time? You almost look pretty in this tape." Or they'd call me after a casting director had given feedback on an audition that they liked me but were going a different direction, and they'd tell me to take time off and go to acting school. Sometimes when I suggested parts I'd found that I thought I was right for, I'd get emails back saying things like, "No, they need someone with sex appeal for that part," or "The director wants someone who can really act," or "Your face isn't right for that one." Sometimes they'd call just to tell me about their weekend in Mexico doing cocaine and cheating on their girlfriends. They'd have me on conference and would talk to each other about all the hookers they'd ordered to the house they'd rented. I'd just sit there on the other end of the line feeling lucky that they'd called me at all.

When I turned twenty they called me to tell me that I should start lying about my age. "People just look at you differently once you hit the twenty mark. We should say you're nineteen for the next couple of years. We'll change your résumé, but if people ask, you're nineteen, okay?"

At the time, it all seemed normal to me. I had an agent, I was starting my career, I should be grateful.

They got me some auditions. The first one they ever sent me on was held in an abandoned wing of a VA psychiatric hospital. I got lost trying to find the office and ended up searching the most definitely haunted halls of the psych ward for far too long. I drove an hour once for an audition they said was for an *American Pie* prequel, but when I got to the waiting room, it became clear it was just a porno by the same name.

They got me jobs sometimes too. I booked a sizzle reel once for a kind of desert noir, kids-on-the-run indie where I was meant to play a girl who couldn't talk, on the lam with her manic pixie dream girl best friend. The girl they cast across from me gave "unhinged" a new name. There was a scene where she was meant to playfully tap my cheek; instead, she slashed my face with her nails. I looked like I got into a bar fight with Wolverine for a week. When I told my agents, they said everyone thought that actress was about to blow up and asked what I had done to provoke her.

There was one exception to the frat boy crew who represented me: my television agent. He handled everything TV-related, and I adored him. He was sweet and thoughtful and I felt like he actually believed in me. He always called me back. He sent me on interesting auditions, good auditions, and some of which I actually booked. He told me what a good job I was doing. He's the one who got me *Girls* and I am forever grateful to him. I truly believe that without this man I wouldn't have the career I have today. I always thought of him as my guardian angel. And to be totally honest, he was the only reason that I stayed at the agency for as long as I did. Well, that and the fear that nobody else would want me.

One day, after season one of *Girls*, I went to the office for a visit. The meeting was vanilla enough that I don't remember it at all, and I said goodbye to my father's agent and the others, while the coke-addicted, cheating one walked me through the cubicle pit of over-worked assistants to the elevators. Halfway there, I stopped to ask him about an indie project I'd emailed them about a few times. A friend of mine was producing it, and it somehow had funding, and there was a role in it, a really, really good role, that I was perfect for. I wasn't a shoo-in for it, but if I slayed the audition, my friend had said, he thought I had a good shot. I needed my agents to email to set up my appointment. And I'd written them about it twice to no response. So I said something like, "Oh hey, did you get my email about that indie film?"

It was like a bomb went off—like I'd poked the coked-up bear right in the funny bone. Standing in front of essentially the entire agency for everyone to see and hear, he started screaming at me. He told me to stop being so annoying and ungrateful and to focus on jobs that were actually real and stop chasing indie films that didn't exist. He told me to stop nagging and to stay in my lane and let them do their jobs. He screamed at me for a solid five minutes. The entire floor had gone silent. Other than his nasal howling, you could hear a pin drop. It was like an episode of bad reality TV, or good reality TV, I suppose, and nobody could take their eyes off us.

I willed myself not to cry, instead just standing there and taking it. And then, as quickly as he had gone off, he switched back to saccharine agent mode and told me how nice it was to see me and that we had to do it more often, and then he shepherded me to the elevator and shoved me in and pressed the button for the garage. I rode down the twenty-some-odd floors in a total daze. But by the time I got to my car I knew what I had to do.

I pulled out onto Santa Monica Boulevard and started driving home. At my first red light, I picked up my phone and dialed the agency. The operator answered and I asked to speak to my father's agent, who by that point had become "mine," which basically meant his name was on my list of contacts on IMDb, not that he actually did anything for me career-wise. I loved that man like an uncle, or at least

I thought I did. We had had holidays together, he'd come over for Shabbat dinner, he loved my father, and my father loved him. I felt like he protected me, like he watched over me, like he wanted for me what I wanted for myself.

When he picked up, I told him what had happened. There was silence on the other end of the phone. So I kept going. I told him I was so grateful for everything he had done for me but that I was leaving the agency, that I didn't think it was the right fit for me anymore, that I needed to go somewhere that I felt welcome.

Again, it was like I had flicked the switch on a killer robot. He went from silence to a rage that made my phone hot. He told me I was an ungrateful little bitch. He told me he had made me and without him I would deflate to nothingness. He told me I was nothing but my last name, and that it was all I had. He told me I was talentless and ugly and that I would never work in this town again, and that he would make sure of it. And then he hung up.

A few months later, I signed with new agents and a manager I am still with today—a group of women I adore more than words, who I know believe in me, who truly want me to succeed, and who love me just as much as a human as they do as an actress. My litmus when I was searching for my new team was, Who would I be okay being trapped in a snowed in cabin in the woods with for a week? I wanted to know they were people I could have fun with and that we would work well together in a crisis. And when I met this group I knew we'd have an epic time.

I never heard from the boys on my team again. My father stayed with his agent, their bond being too strong to break. I understood that. The entertainment industry does funny things to loyalty, blurring the lines when money and power and success are involved. Years after that phone call, I ran into the agent at a premiere of my father's. I was about four seasons into *Girls*, and the show had become a massive hit. I still couldn't get a job when the show wasn't filming and was hustling my ass off to try to create work beyond the show, but I was happy. I was working on something special with people I loved and was playing a part I adored. Things were good.

We had all gathered in New York for the premiere. It was a nice night. The movie was great, the party was fun, it was the holidays, and New York was showing off with its Christmas splendor. I was getting a Diet Coke from the bar when I turned around, and there he was, my father's agent. Standing far too close to me, as if he'd been stalking me, waiting for this moment. He was drunk. And he was ANGRY. There was a hatred in his eyes, like he'd been nursing a grudge ever since that phone call, and it had festered into a growth that he had to excise somehow, and he believed the only way to get it out was to spew it at me.

He started to poke me in the chest with his pointer finger, hard. So hard that it backed me up. "I hope you're enjoying your success," he said. "I hope you're fucking enjoying the success that I created for you," he said. "I fucking made you," he said as he poked me harder and harder.

He went on from there, continuing to poke me and back me up until I was finally up against a wall. He told me I owed him everything and I was an ungrateful brat and that without him I never would have gotten so much as a Chipotle commercial, and that everyone knew I stole this from him, as if somehow he was the one on-screen actually playing my part. He was so angry I felt sad for him, sad that he'd carried this around, that a girl a third his age had caused him so much strife. Eventually my husband saw me from across the room and realized what was happening and came to pry him off of me. It took me a second for the shock to wear off, but once it did I just started sobbing.

To this day I don't totally understand why he hated me so much, why all those boys did. But I walked away from that night with the validation that I had obviously made the right decision.

Years passed. Life went on. Work went on. And I never really heard his name. My father didn't talk to me about him; we just left that alone. And then, one day, he screwed my dad over. They'd been friends for over twenty years. They'd worked together for even longer. And on a deal for a movie, a run-of-the-mill deal that ended up falling through, instead of supporting his dear friend and client of multiple decades, this guy decided to make a little bit of money and side with the shady investors instead. (Who, by the way, ended up screwing him over in the end too. So he was out one of his biggest clients, one of his oldest friends, and the money he'd picked over it all. Just goes to show you: karma's a bitch.)

There will always be men like this in my industry, in every industry, in the world, because we have created a safe space for them to grow and thrive. They rule with fear and they're effective because they grow so big we think they are beyond conquering. But at the end of the day, they're mostly smoke and mirrors.

Ultimately, I used the word my father taught me is the most powerful thing you can say in Hollywood: NO. I told him no, and I walked away. And he puffed up his chest and probably told anyone who would listen that I was a nepo hack, and they shouldn't hire me, which, you know what, is fine.

Because in the end, at least this time, I got the last laugh.

RADIOHEAD AND
KURT VONNEGUT

Do you know who Kurt Vonnegut is?"
    I nod tentatively even though of course I know who Kurt
Vonnegut is.

"He's one of my favorite authors . . ."

He pauses for dramatic effect, I assume. And then he says . . .

"I fucked his daughter too."

He's still inside me. If you can even really call it that. His dick is the
size of a lipstick.

I'd met him at a street fair about a week before. I was there with
two guy friends, not looking for anything other than a hot dog I could
pretend to eat and a good time with my friends. But he sauntered up
and he knew my buddy so we got to talking. He immediately seemed
like one of those guys who lives life like a Bukowski novel, like he was
curating his life "through the lens of" a cool young artist.

"Hey."

"Hey."

"I'm a friend of X."

"Well, a friend of X is a friend of mine."

"You're cute."

"Why, thank you."

"I'm an artist."

"Cool, what kind of art?"

"I mean, what not kind of art. I don't bullshit, brilliance. Art, man, I make art. Hey, what if I just asked you out. Like right now? Like what if I just did that?"

He came on strong. I mean, he came on exceptionally strong. So strong that it almost wasn't.

Very Bukowski.

"Are you asking me out?"

He was. I accepted. I gave him my number and the next day he texted me and asked if I wanted to go see Radiohead at the Hollywood Bowl.

Yes, yes I did. I lived in Santa Monica. He lived in Silver Lake, so I drove to his house and he cooked for me. He was making pasta with clams. I didn't eat pasta or clams. At this point in my life I didn't really eat anything at all, but I was too embarrassed to tell him that. Hey, ready for our hot date? By the way I won't be eating because I starve myself on a daily basis. Isn't that sexy?!

As he cooked he went on about how a very old man off the coast of a very old small island had taught him how to make this very old, very special recipe just so. Nobody else in the greater Los Angeles area knew how to make this very simple yet also exceptionally complicated pasta with clams, because nobody else had known this old magical man. (The secret was something to do with using forks to separate the pasta as it boiled.) There were lots of steps, so many steps, and lots and lots of some kind of sweet wine that I really didn't care for but again didn't want to be rude so drank anyway. And I'm not entirely sure how, but I managed to pretend to eat without actually eating any of the pasta with clams.

His house was insane. He either came from money or was actually as successful an artist as he claimed to be or both.

"I have galleries in New York and Amsterdam and I'm talking to one in Paris."

I didn't know a lot about art, but he explained to me that it's all about your galleries. And that he'd recently sold a painting for twenty thousand dollars. So that explained his massively sized, sparsely decorated, very expensive-looking and -smelling house on a very hidden and seemingly elite street in Silver Lake.

After dinner, he drove us to the Hollywood Bowl. Just as we pulled into the parking lot filled with parking attendants who always look as if they've (a) never done this before, (b) don't know what a car is or how to drive, and (c) want to kill themselves and everyone around them, he screamed "FUCK" at the top of his lungs.

"I forgot the fucking tickets. We have to go back."

So go back we did. He'd left them by the front door. (God, remember paper tickets for things? How inconvenient.) Anyway, we righted his wrong and found ourselves back where we'd started at the Hollywood Bowl again. But this time running late. Now the parking attendants all looked like they'd just given birth to triplets and didn't know which way was up or if they cared enough to muster the energy to keep on breathing because it was all just too hard and their tanks were empty.

"Well, I guess we have to valet. Fuck. That's gonna cost me an arm and a leg."

I'm sure valet isn't cheap, but I thought, Didn't you just sell a twenty-thousand-dollar painting?

Anyway, we handed the car over, and he whisked me into the bowl down into our exceptionally good seats.

Throughout the entire Radiohead set, he groped and caressed and prodded and grinded onto any part of me he could find.

I didn't care. I had fallen into a vortex of joy. I was stone-cold sober but felt like I was tripping.

The light show alone would have been enough to send me over the edge. The artistry that went into creating a visual reference for the sound they coated our bodies and minds with was almost too much. But there was also a seamlessness to the entire show. Like they incepted your brain from the moment they struck their first melancholic chord and then held you there in the matrix of their brilliance until the last song.

When the concert ended I just stood there for a while, coming down, feeling as if they had licked the inside of my veins and left behind a sticky joy-inducing residue. I've never done heroin but I imagine the sensation is similar.

So too, I imagine, is the comedown.

The guy collected his car from valet and we sat in the classic hour-long gridlock of the bowl parking lot until eventually we made it back to his Silver Lake enclave, where we had sex. It was sloppy and boring and fast.

At this point, I should mention that earlier in the date, he told me that my father was "one of my idols" or "one of my favorite authors of all time" or something else equally weird and annoying to hear on a first date. But whatever, I'm used to it.

But, as we were lying there postcoital, he asked if I know who Kurt Vonnegut was. (I know this is a replay, but it's really the punch line, so just humor me.) So I nodded. And he said, "He's one of my favorite authors . . . I fucked his daughter too."

My immediate reaction was to giggle, which is what I normally do when I am immensely and overwhelmingly uncomfortable. But some higher power caught the laugh in my throat, and instead, I just stared at him with my jaw hanging loose. And I wished upon a star that I somehow had heard him wrong.

I actually met Kurt Vonnegut's daughter years later at a party. I told her what had happened to me and we shared a cringe and a chuckle. She told me what a piece of shit he'd been to her, how all he'd talked about was her father and his overpriced art. She asked if he'd made me the pasta. I told her he had. We agreed the old man from the small island didn't exist and the clams were probably canned.

One might think this is where the story ends. But sadly, it's not.

I made my exit gracefully but swiftly after that delightful little speech of his. But somehow, in my haste I FORGOT MY FUCKING FAVORITE, STAPLE-OF-MY-CLOSET, WEAR-EVERY-DAY-SINCE-I'M-FIFTEEN leather jacket. And I didn't realize it until I got home. All the way to Santa Monica.

I get it. I know you're thinking, Ohhhhh, okay. You "FORGOT" your jacket. No. I was never, have never been, will never be (I mean, I'm married now, so that would be weird, but I'm MAKING A POINT!) one of those girls! Also, I loved that jacket more than anything. I would NEVER leave it behind intentionally. I found it at the Rose Bowl flea market when I was fifteen. I bought it for forty dollars and never looked back. And I had left it at "Do you know who Kurt Vonnegut is?"'s house. Like a fucking idiot . . .

So the next day . . .

"Hey. I left my leather jacket at your house, can I come by and get it tonight?"

"Fine. But you have to come on the earlier side because I have to be up early. I have a pus-filled boil on my ass that I'm having extracted in the morning so I have to get a good night's sleep."

He had to be kidding, right?

No.

I get there. Classical music is blasting. He's smoking a cigarette and isn't wearing a shirt.

He starts to download me about the boil. How much it hurts. How intense the extraction will be. How big it is. How much pus they might find. The decision of whether or not to keep it. How emotionally challenging the whole experience has been. I think at some point his mother came up but I've blocked that out. Protective function.

Just a note here. The sex the night before had been fast, but this golf-ball-sized boil he was describing had not been in evidence from what I could tell.

Anyway. He goes on and on about it while also telling me I really need to go and it's kind of a bummer that I've come over and interrupted his presurgery evening's rest because he really needs to be calm and collected and fresh for the pus extraction tomorrow and that I really need to go but also one more thing about the boil and another twenty minutes of let me tell you and also do I want to see it?

I do not.

I do not want to see it.

I do not want to see him.

I kind of want to punch him in his lipstick dick and then put his cigarette out in his boil and leave him for dead, but instead I just run out of his overly underdecorated Silver Lake mansion clutching my beloved leather jacket to my chest and I don't stop until I reach the safety of my car. And then I speed home and shower and take an Ambien and sleep the sleep of the dead, attempting to erase the experience into my slumber and hopefully wake up the next morning confused and thinking it was a fever dream.

Afterward, I never felt angry or used or even really upset about the situation. It was mostly just bizarre. But I did feel grateful. Terrible, potentially (at least momentarily) traumatizing experience aside, I got to see FUCKING RADIOHEAD at the HOLLYWOOD FUCK-ING BOWL so close to the stage I swear I could taste their sweat in my mouth. So, all things considered, I'd say what happened was worth it. For Radiohead. And the story.

I never saw that guy ever again. I wonder where he is now. Trying to fuck other authors' daughters or in Paris selling paintings? Maybe his ass boils finally took him down. Who's to say? The universe works in mysterious ways.

I gave that leather jacket away a few years ago during a closet cleanout. It finally felt like time. I was worried I'd regret it but I don't, not one bit.

I don't regret any of it.

DEPRESSION

It's a pain in my chest like my lungs have gone down a size. Or actually, it feels like they lost weight and bought new jeans to fit their slender frame, and then gained the weight back from melancholy and laziness and lack of self-worth, and now they're trying to squeeze back into their skinny jeans and they don't fit.

I can't breathe. My lungs are heavy. And the heaviness pulls the rest of me down with it. I envision my feet being pulled down through the hardwood floors, sinking into the wood as they splinter, the force of the sadness pulling me down, down, down into the earth.

I search for whatever it is that will make this stop. That damned key that I put somewhere safe so I wouldn't lose it. The one that you click into the spot and turn to make me stop crying uncontrollably.

I can't find it.

I don't want to do anything. My entire sensory palate has turned beige and nothing excites it. I'm hungry but I don't want to eat. I make eggs and toast and just stare at them. I drink more coffee. And more and more, which certainly isn't helping.

Doing, feeling, consuming, I don't want any of it. I only want to fix what is broken in me. To stop these feelings. To exorcise myself.

Yes, that's what I need, an exorcism. But where does one even find one of those these days? Craigslist? Google? I'm too tired to search and how would I know if they were good and then if it didn't work THEN where would I be? Out one exorcism and still nowhere to go but down.

I hate that I am here in—this place I know so well and fight so hard to avoid.

If you've never experienced depression before, it's like this: Think of a town you pass on your way to somewhere, perhaps on a regular commute. A place you see through the driver's-side window as you travel toward your much better, happier destination.

As you pass, you think, I wonder who lives in that town. I'm glad I don't. Because nobody leaves there, nobody graduates, everybody fights with their spouse and people die alone in that town. Thank god I'm on my way to somewhere else, you think as you pass it by. Thank god I don't live in that town.

And then one day as you pass you realize you're out of gas.

You have to stop there.

You have no other option but to stop there.

And so you do. And the man who pumps your gas starts to talk to you. And before you know it, before you realize it, you've spent an hour there. And you're late for that other place, that happier, better place. But the streets of this town are confusing and unmarked. You try to find the highway, the one that will take you back to the path you were on before, but you end up driving in circles. And then it gets dark and you realize you'll have to stay the night. So you buy a toothbrush and a man's T-shirt to sleep in. You rent a room at the only motel. You stay the night.

And then, without even realizing it, a second night passes. And then another. And soon, you live there.

You do not like this town. You never feel comfortable or good or proud of your existence there. You do not want to stay, but leaving feels somehow impossible. Every day you wake up there you think,

Today is the day I leave. But then the hours pass and the sun rises and sets and as you ready yourself for bed you think, Tomorrow, tomorrow is the day that I leave. And again and again and tomorrow and tomorrow and the more that time passes the firmer your feet cement to the ground.

It is not desire that finally motivates you leaving. It is a deep exhausted frustration, an inner disgust for who you are in this place, for who you have become, for the version of you that lives in this town. And that disgust morphs into momentum. And finally, one day, it is no longer tomorrow. And finally, you get out of that town. But the muscle memory of it stays inside you forever.

Sometimes, without meaning to, you pull off the highway to that stop.

Or sometimes your feet walk you back there.

And then you are there. With your toothbrush in a motel room, staring at a map and trying to find your way out again.

SCARS

My body came online slowly. Bits and pieces one by one. My hips, my shoulders, my back. Rebooting, rebooting, rebooting. The fog coating my brain was still thick, like it had been submerged in a bathtub filled with honey. But there was enough awareness there to clock the pain.

I was naked. I was on the floor covered with a throw blanket or a towel or maybe an unzipped hoodie haphazardly thrown over my bare body. Everything hurt. Every single piece of me screamed out in protest as I felt more and more. I wasn't eating at this point in my life, and my skeletal frame advertised the signs of what it looks like to sleep on a hard floor when you're actually skin and bones. I was covered in bruises, deep throbbing ones that hurt without even touching them.

Hips, elbows, ribs. I was the color of a magenta sky.

I slowly took stock of the damage. Like the stupid fucking body scans they make you do in a yoga class in an attempt to relax into yourself when all you really want is a Percocet and a joint. Feel your feet, are they broken, no. Feel your hands, do you have all ten fingers, yes. And so on.

I couldn't open my eyes yet; they were too heavy. I tried to remember where I was, I tried to remember what had happened. You know those anxiety dreams where someone is chasing you and you try to run but your legs feel like they're moving through quicksand or water or something sticky? That's what my brain felt like. But I kept pushing it, making my way from the depths back to the surface of reality.

And then he spoke and everything snapped into a violently sharp focus.

"Good morning, sunshine! Would you like some coffee?"

I sat up like a jack-in-the-box. Pain erupted throughout my body and I thought I was going to be sick. The blanket or hoodie or whatever was covering me fell away for a moment, and as I reached down to grab it and cover myself, I saw the dried flaking blood caking the inside of my thighs all the way down to my knees.

This is what I remember.

The club door. The people I called friends at the time knew the bouncer. We skipped the line. It was a dark, loud, warehouse-sized room with a center dance floor lined with couches and booths that cost thousands of dollars to sit on and were probably covered with coke and bodily fluids and mixers and who knows what diseases. We took up residence in two of them. We drank overpriced vodka and danced on the tables and a friend of a friend of someone who knew someone else grabbed me and lifted my ninety pounds up with one arm, telling me I was the size of an Olsen twin. And then somewhere within the timeless haze of the club, he emerged, and he smiled and he asked if he could buy me a drink. I said sure and he walked me over to the corner bar so we could "talk."

I remember his face, his smile, how nerdy and safe he seemed. I remember him handing me my drink and taking a sip through that tiny red straw.

And then I don't remember.

It's black, it's an abyss. There is absolute nothingness within the void of the time lost. But then there are flashes. They're barely there, they are a whisper, an insult to the word memory.

It goes like this.

There is a black hole.

And then there is the cab.

I am melted wax. I am amorphous. My bones feel loose and malleable and warm.

Then there is nothing again.

An apartment. His bed. My bones are no longer loose; they simply aren't there. I am buried alive. It is as if cement has been poured into my mouth, making its way through every inch of my body, not yet hardened but close to setting. He is stripping off my clothing. And this is something most people won't believe given my detailed description of being physically and mentally incapacitated, but:

I said no.

I said no over and over and over again. It wasn't loud or strong and it may have come out as a mumbled whisper. But I fucking said it.

And then the black hole engulfs me and there is nothing.

Until I wake up naked, bloody, bruised on the floor of his apartment and he offers me coffee.

Here's where it gets really fucked up.

I say yes.

And we have coffee on his balcony. And he talks at me for the next few hours and he smiles and pecks my cheek, and to an outsider you would think this was a cute new couple having a happy Sunday morning hang.

I don't remember what I said. To be honest, I'm not sure I said anything. He was a narcissist, so I'm not sure he would have noticed or cared if I was entirely mute. But I sat there and listened. I didn't scream or run or punch him in the nuts. I didn't confront him. I did absolutely nothing.

Then he asked if he could walk me back to my hotel. And I let him. And when we got to the lobby he kissed me goodbye and said he'd call me.

A few weeks later he texted me asking for my address in Los Angeles, which I sent to him. To which he mailed a copy of his *New York Times* bestselling book. Which, you guessed it, I fucking read. To be completely honest, it wasn't bad.

And then he came to LA on business and asked if he could see me. And yet again, I agreed. I picked him up at his hotel in Hollywood and I don't remember what we did but I'll never forget his face when he got into my car. He was beaming, he was fucking jolly, he thought we were courting. I guess, in a way, we were.

I never saw him or spoke to him again after that trip to LA. He texted me a few times but I stopped responding. He faded into the background of my memories. Not forgotten but just not important enough to exist among the breathing memories.

I googled him before I wrote this. He looks exactly the same, but what strikes me now is how entirely ordinary he looks. He never wrote another book. I didn't dig deep, but it looks like he didn't do much with his life either.

I wonder where that lost time went. Somewhere with the lost socks that disappear in the dryer, perhaps? Like Schrödinger's cat, do those seconds and hours and minutes exist or was I truly floating within a void? A sensory deprivation chamber of my own existence brought on by a semi-cute bespectacled narcissist and the spiked vodka tonic he bought me in order to get laid?

Now here's the really, truly fucked-up part. Even if he hadn't drugged me, I probably would have fucked him anyway. I was young and damaged and hated myself. At the time, I didn't really care what happened to me. I was a depressed, anorexic, anxious lump of brain matter existing within a meat suit that I couldn't even look at in the mirror. If he'd asked me to go home with him, I more than likely would have said yes.

But you know, I guess everyone likes a sure bet. And what's a roofie other than a foolproof insurance policy?

Why didn't I run out of his apartment that morning? Why did I let him serve me coffee and walk me home? Why did I read his goddamn book? Why the fuck did I see him again?

I've tried to answer these questions and I can't. I don't know. The entire experience feels shot full of Novocain. And no matter how hard I try the numbness never seems to wear off.

I do not think about this time in my life often. I do not think about this man often. This isn't an active choice or an act of suppression, it's just not something that defines me. I like to think that I am who I am today because of all these things that happened to me, not in spite of them. Our scars tell a story; they are a map of where we have been.

One of my favorite folktales is about scars. It goes like this: When you die, you are ferried across a river to the golden land of the afterlife. Awaiting you on the shore is a monster who inspects your naked body when you arrive. If you have scars, he lets you through to live out the rest of your days in the land of milk and honey. If you do not have scars, he eats you.

Sometimes, when the sun is shining the brightest and my husband is smiling at me with a face filled with love and the world around me is calm and good, I will suddenly feel a wash of fear or sadness. The only feeling I can really equate it to is homesickness or nostalgia. It feels sharp, like when you swallow something bubbly too fast. I feel it in my chest. I think it is because I can't fully comprehend the goodness that my life has become. And there's always the overwhelming fear that I do not deserve it and that the moment I allow myself to truly enjoy it, it will all go away. And so when it all hits me too hard, I find one of those scars and I touch it.

I feel lucky that I made it past the darkness I used to reside in. And then I think about the girl that I was. The pill-popping, emaciated, self-hating, hollow-souled girl. I want to embrace her and hold her and tell her that she will move past the emotional tidal wave she is under. I want to tell her that her life will be filled with happiness and that she will be loved by so many people. That she will marry the love of her life—a wonderful man who will be good to her, who will make her feel worthy and safe. That she won't be this tired forever. That she will learn how to say no.

I want to tell her that I know these experiences hurt, that they are cutting deep into her in places she didn't even know existed, but that the cuts will heal, and that they will form into beautiful scars, scars that will be her ticket to the promised land.

THE TAMPON DISPENSER IS A PROP

I'm in it. The eighth circle of hell. There is no escape. There is no bargaining your way out of it. This is my life now. It's been ninety minutes and I've moved half a city block. I am in my car, in a traffic jam on the 10 freeway, headed downtown, on a Friday afternoon. I'm fucked.

Los Angeles traffic is like constipation. It is just part of being alive. And there are only two ways to deal with it: suffer through it until it eventually releases you from its torturous hell grip or plow through it with a Mack truck. And if you're wondering, What is the Mack truck analogy for constipation? I'm thinking colonic, but you can fill in the blank if you disagree.

Why am I driving into the bowels of hell at the absolute worst time on the absolute worst day of the week, you ask? Well, I have an audition today. And if you aren't familiar with the desperation of a working (or, Please, baby Jesus, let me be a working) actor, let me give you the CliffsNotes:

We will do basically anything for a job or even the prospect of one.

For example: a few hypotheticals for you . . .

At 9:00 p.m. on a Thursday night, you get a call for an audition. It's for 9:00 a.m. the next morning. It's fifteen pages of dialogue, which mostly consist of your character monologuing. No problem at all, you just drink twenty-seven shots of espresso and stay up the entire night learning the lines.

You get a job in a summer rom-com about a bathing-suit designer, but it films in Siberia, for tax break purposes. So the shoot is entirely exteriors, in bikinis. Whatever! Frostbite will make for a great story on *Late Night*, and who needs all their toes anyway?! From an evolutionary standpoint those appendages aren't necessary!

You've studied for weeks for a huge audition. It's a serious role, a real meaty part, something you can really sink your teeth into and show your range. They've asked for a Russian accent. There are notes in your appointment sheet about how important the accent is, how if you can nail this accent the part is essentially yours. So you work for hours every day running the lines; you hire a dialect coach with money you don't really have to help you make the accent seem seamless, natural, beautiful. En route to your audition you get a call from your agent that they've changed the accent. Now they want Australian, so can you do that instead.

They want full nudity? Sure, why not.

They're deferring payment. I mean, the part is great, so okay.

It's six-day weeks. That's fine, I'll sleep when I'm dead.

You have to show up and be perfect, be off book but ready to improv but only if they tell you to. Have sex appeal but not too much cause you'll seem slutty. Be nice but not too talkative 'cause they could get annoyed. Be on time but not too early because that's weird but not one minute late because that's disrespectful. Show you love the part but don't NEED it. And whatever you do, do not seem desperate. Slay the audition but don't act cocky. Be confident but not so much that you seem like you're above direction. And for the love of everything holy, somehow, within this delicate, impossible dance, make yourself seem like the one they should give the job to.

That's why I am sitting in paralytic, backwards-moving downtown Los Angeles traffic on a Friday afternoon. Because I have a fucking audition. It is my first and only one in weeks, if you don't count the one I had the week before for an Xbox webisode called "The Uzi

Journal"—I know what you're thinking: real Oscar bait, that one. Don't get too excited—I didn't get it.

But other than that, it has been crickets on the audition front. Granted, it had been August. And in August the industry slows down to a pace that makes a snail look like Seabiscuit thanks to all the studio execs running away to wherever their yachts are docked. It is a month right after the summer blockbusters have blockbustered and before the fall awards contenders start contending and so everyone powers down because there is seemingly nothing for them to do. And the rest of us are left to twiddle our thumbs and wait for the people who schedule the auditions and green-light the movies to return with their, for once, real tans.

But now it is September, which, as far as I understand, is not August but rather an entirely different month, so I'd been hoping for a change of pace. Sadly, no such luck.

Until today. Because I have an audition, and it isn't for a video game or a training video for a yogurt packaging plant or a student film about chlamydia. It's for a real television show. This, my friends, is not a drill.

My audition is downtown at the Los Angeles Center Studios, an actor's nightmare. It's a beautiful old retro building the size of Texas, with individual elevators for every different floor and endless window-less hallways that all look the same. The parking structure is an entirely different kind of clusterfuck with switchbacks and confusing signs and dead ends. You need twenty minutes just to figure out how to enter the place.

I have always given myself two hours to get to an audition. Just in case. I live in fear of being late. If I'm there fifteen minutes before I'm supposed to be, I'm already sweating. Today, I have given myself three hours because I knew the 10 would fuck me over like a hedge fund guy with a Ponzi scheme. And still, I am cutting it close.

Sitting in the traffic, I can see downtown LA, I can smell it, it is sooooo close—if only these thousands of cars would move out of the way. I bang my steering wheel and scream at the top of my lungs. (One of the benefits of living in LA and constantly traveling about in these tiny bubbles: You can do things that are normally totally unacceptable public behavior, like screeching "FUCK" into the abyss, and nobody cares or really notices. Because they're all doing the same thing in their little bubbles.) The scream gives me a tickle in my throat, which makes me sneeze.

And then, I get my fucking period.

I'm sure it was coming with or without the sneeze, but something about the sneeze seems to coax it out of me.

After a prolonged history with an eating disorder, in the past, my period has come late, then not come at all for many years, and then as of late, come so erratically that it is anyone's best guess when it will touch down. But, lucky girl that I am, it has chosen today of all days, the day of my audition.

I was wearing extremely tight high-waisted bell-bottom jeans that you can really only wear with a specific type of underwear that I only had one pair of and couldn't find while I was racing to get ready so I'd opted to just go commando. Again, lucky fucking me.

Now I'll also say the unpredictability of my period was not limited to timing but also severity. Sometimes it was a whisper, other times it was a goddamn monsoon. Today, it happened to be the latter.

I stare down at my crotch watching a glorious stain spread, simultaneously trying to keep an eye on the road and frantically searching my car for something, anything, to plug up the hole in my body that was currently leaking. Obviously this is when the sea of traffic decides to magically clear up. So now I'm going ninety down the 10 trying not to be late, trying not to bleed through my jeans or stain the seat of my car, and really trying so fucking hard not to cry and ruin my makeup that took me an hour to do because truly who actually knows how to do a cat eye that's even on both sides?!

I find an old napkin in the center console and I shove it down my pants with one hand as I drive with the other. I find a parking spot within the maze of the lot, walk two steps, and already can't find my car. This place is Brigadoon. Trying to be resourceful, I decide to pull a Hansel and Gretel and make an Altoids trail from my car to the elevator, but I run out of mints halfway through and the Listerine strips dissolve on the concrete, so I give up. Whatever, I'll walk home. I've come this far and I just need a fucking bathroom.

I spill out of the elevator into the lobby, searching for a sign, bathroom, restrooms, women, I don't care, something, anything that can help. I see nothing so I beeline for the doorman.

"Bathroom?!"

He looks at me like I'm something unpleasant that washed up on shore. He tells me there aren't any bathrooms in the lobby and makes me sign in and get a guest badge, then directs me to the proper elevator. "There are bathrooms on the floor you're going to," he tells me. Okay, I'm almost there. One more elevator ride. I scurry across the lobby as quickly as I can, which isn't quick at all. I'm walking like I have precious jewels hidden up my vagina, squeezing as tightly as I can trying to mitigate the damage.

The elevator dings for my floor, I burst out, and I see it. Twenty feet from the elevator: a RESTROOM sign. I run. Well, I scuttle, still squeezing my thighs together. I mutter under my breath a prayer to a god I don't believe in that if he just gets me through this with minimal to no embarrassment and possibly a job at the end, I promise I'll never leave the house without a tampon again and I'll never swear or speed or wish girls who got the parts I wanted would end up on a very nice but totally remote and deserted island never to be seen again.

I shove open the door to the women's room and fucking A, there it is right before me. Like the holy grail, like manna in the desert, like water in the . . . well, desert too, I guess: a tampon dispenser.

I've never been so excited to see a white metal box filled with hot-dog-shaped cotton. And thank god I stocked up on quarters before I left the house. I grab a handful out of my bag and go to line them up in the slots in order to get my prize, but there's a problem. The quarters don't fit.

I look closer; it says five cents. The machine wants nickels. But I don't have nickels. The tampons are a brand I had never heard of. BED-FELLOWS, A LADY'S BEST FRIEND is plastered on the front in what looks like an ad out of a fifties magazine. What is happening?

I try hopelessly to fit my quarters into the nickel-sized slots. Then I try banging on the machine in a classic I-don't-have-change-but-if-I-just-hit-the-vending-machine-maybe-it-will-give-me-the-snack-I-want move, but other than hurting my hand, nothing happens.

I start to cry. Actually, I start to sob. My makeup is fucked, my nose is snotty, I'm late for my audition, and I'm bleeding through my favorite jeans. In short, my life is over.

Just as my sobs really start to kick up a notch and I decide to try taking the dispenser off the wall, a woman comes into the bathroom, witnessing me in all my glory. I turn to her, most likely looking insane. She looks at me, my fist full of quarters, bloodstain on my crotch, general look of utter dismay, and sighs.

"Oh, honey. Are you trying to use the machine?" she says.

All I can muster is a nod.

"It's a prop. They shot a scene here. This happens about once a month. I keep telling them to take it down or switch it out."

Right. Of course. They film *Mad Men* here. This is a fake tampon dispenser, one that Betty Draper most likely stood in front of applying her lipstick. There probably aren't even any tampons in there. Was Bedfellows even a brand of tampon? IS ANYTHING REAL?! The woman looks at me with such pity, I want to punch her Good Samaritan face. She asks if I need a tampon and again, I just nod. She goes away and comes back with two. I sit in the stall by myself for a good ten minutes trying to camouflage the stain in my jeans and waiting for the tears to pass. Then I go to sign in for my audition.

The room is full, and they are obviously running horribly behind because the girl helping with the sign-in process looks like she wants to exit the planet. She picks a group of five of us and whisks us into a different waiting room, which is right outside the casting director's office. There is only one other girl there reading for the same part; the rest are old men hoping to be cast as Police Officer #4. The sign-in girl runs into the casting director's office and informs him that Hannah (I suppose that was the other girl's name) had arrived.

"Oh, uh, have her read with John, you know, have John read the girls, and if they're good, send 'em in here."

John is the assistant, if you can even call him that. John answers phones and puts stickies on things. I tell John he can call me Z instead of Zosia because most people find it easier, and he just stares at me like I am speaking in tongues.

"Z, like zebra, or the last letter in the alphabet?" I try to explain.

"I'm sorry, I don't understand," John says.

Okay, John, whatever.

John reads Hannah and then sends her into the casting director's office. Hannah is in there for-fucking-ever. When she finally leaves, John comes out for me and we step into the hallway to "run the scene."

We do it once, and John just looks at me. Exasperated.

"Okay, uh . . . well, um—"

(He is clearly searching for my name and just can't find it or the one letter option I gave him in that noggin of his.)

"—that was . . . good, but could you make the middle of the scene more of an argument?"

"You want me to argue with her?"

"No, don't argue with her. Just make it an argument."

"Oh, okay, the whole middle section?"

"No, just that one line."

"You want me to make just one line an argument?"

"Yes."

"Okay. Um. Okay. Which line?"

"You know."

Okay, John, whatever you want. At this point I just want to go home and crawl down my bathroom drain and turn into a tadpole and die.

But we do the scene again. I do it the same exact way.

After the second time, John says, "Well . . . I guess, thank you . . . for uh . . . coming in."

And that is it. I don't make the cut, don't even get to see the casting director. Just John. John who is deciding my fate as an actress for today.

I eventually find my car.

Rush hour has now ended, so I get home in under thirty minutes.

The stain will never fully come out of these jeans but I'll figure out how to make it acceptable enough so that I can keep wearing them.

Going forward, I still forget to keep tampons in my bag.

Oh, and I don't get that job.

But I guess at least it makes for a good story?

Oh, Hollywood . . .

MR. OZ

I can't find my scissors so we're gonna have to use a straight razor."

It's six in the morning. I'm sitting in a makeup trailer in downtown LA in a parking lot next to the river. I've landed a recurring role on one of the biggest shows currently on television. The kind of show that's a phenomenon, that makes people fall in love with TV as a medium all over again. I never thought I'd get this job. When I went to the audition I honestly thought I was just there for fill. So the fact that I'm here already feels like a mistake.

I'd woken up at 3:00 a.m. because I was so terrified of sleeping through the alarm I'd set for 4:00 a.m. because my call time was 6:00 a.m. but I wanted to get there at 5:30 just to be safe. They sat me in the hair chair at 5:55, and just as I sat down, the showrunner's assistant came in and began talking to the head of the hair department like I wasn't there. They both looked at my reflection in the mirror as if it were a photograph.

"I didn't know her hair was that long?" the assistant said.

"Me either," the head hairdresser said.

My hair had always been this long. My hair had never not been this long. In my audition, which the showrunner had attended, in all my fitting photos, in my entire nineteen years of life that I had lived up until now, my hair had always been this long. But they seemed to be upset with me inadvertently for not telling them that my hair was this long. It was below my boobs at this point and, as previously mentioned, had been ever since they met me.

They continued to stare at me in the mirror as the assistant took a photo, texted it to someone, waited for a reply, and then turned to the head hairdresser and said, "He doesn't like it. You need to cut a bob and we need her on set in five for a blocking rehearsal, with short hair."

The blood drained entirely from the body of the hairdresser as if a vampire had tapped her like a keg. And then she snapped to and began to tear the hair and makeup trailer apart searching for her cutting scissors. Three minutes into our five minutes, she gave up her search and held up a straight razor. That's when she told me she couldn't find her scissors and this would have to do. And then, without so much as asking me, she went to work. She grabbed a fistful of my long, thick horse mane of hair and began slicing it Sweeney Todd–style. As it fell around me I just kept thinking, Maybe this is a dream, maybe this is a prank, maybe I never got this part at all and this entire thing has been a hallucination.

Two minutes later I was staring at myself in the mirror with chin-length hair. The rest of it sprawled on the ground around me, missing its host. I could still feel it, almost like a phantom limb. A production assistant came in and whisked me off to set for a blocking rehearsal that I floated through. Nobody mentioned my hair again. Nobody mentioned the length or the fact that it looked like somebody had frantically cut it with a straight razor, which they had.

The first day of shooting was a success, and minus my impromptu haircut, I had a blast. One of the actors on the show was directing for the first time, and he was absolutely incredible at it. And something about the energy of it being his first day at something new put me slightly at ease about waltzing into this overwhelming, successful, and established show as a newbie who had just had a traumatizing 6:00 a.m. haircut with a utensil not meant to cut hair.

I went home at the end of that day having forgotten entirely about how my morning had started until I washed my hair and realized how truly uneven the cut actually was. But it didn't matter, nothing a trim in an actual salon with actual scissors couldn't fix.

I did a couple more episodes of the show that season. And while the nerves didn't entirely wear off and there were still bumps along the road and the other actors definitely kept to themselves quite a bit, it was still a thrill and I loved every second of it.

And I always got along with the crew so well. It turned out the on-set props guy lived a couple blocks from me in Venice, and we became friends and he taught me how to play the ukulele. The costume designer was an absolute tornado of a woman who I came to adore. Her sincerity in her ridiculousness was something I wished I could emulate. When she'd try to put me in a pair of pants I was convinced I wouldn't be able to breathe in and I'd say, "These aren't going to fit," she'd always respond with, "If you can zip 'em, they fit."

And then a glorious thing happened. They asked me to come back and do more episodes for the following season. I was over the moon—how could I be so lucky? I showed up on set for the first episode of the new season ready for anything. If they had asked me to buzz my head I would have been cool with it. If they had asked me to get naked, I probably would have done it. I was ready to roll with whatever they threw at me. Or so I thought.

The show's creator and showrunner was an intense human. He directed some episodes every season but not all of them. This one was being directed by someone else. The showrunner wasn't always around, but when he was, the entire vibe of the set would change, as if a cold front had swept the soundstage. I never entirely understood why. He was definitely spirited and opinionated, but there's way worse than that in Hollywood. I had always thought there was maybe something I was missing.

I was correct.

We were doing a blocking rehearsal when he showed up on set. The scene was short and easy. I was meant to come into the office, tell everyone I had photos of something important, remove them from the manila envelope I was carrying, and place them on the table. Then everyone had a few more lines and that was it. So we're rehearsing, I walk in, I go to take the photos out of the envelope, and the showrunner calls "Cut." Not the director of the episode, the showrunner. And we all look at each other like, Did somebody do something wrong? We all thought the scene was going fine.

He gets up out of his chair at the monitors and walks toward me slowly, looking at the ground the entire time like he's trying to figure out how to word what he's about to say. And when he finally stops right in front of me, he takes a few more beats before he lifts his head, looks at me, and says, "What the fuck are you doing?" To which I say, "Um . . . rehearsing?"

And then he grabs my hand that's holding the manila envelope and he says, "No! What the fuck are you doing with this! That's not how you take something out of an envelope! Do it again!"

So we do it again, and again, and again. And every time we get to the part of the scene where I'm meant to take the photos out of the envelope, he calls "Cut" and he gets up and he yells. Well, first, he starts off just raising his voice, which escalates to yelling, which eventually mutates into full-out screaming.

He spews the kitchen sink at me:

"You're doing it wrong!"

"How the fuck can you think that looks right at all?"

"That's not how anyone would remove anything from an envelope ever!"

"I don't understand—when I cast you, you knew how to act."

"I'm honestly confused at how you can be so bad at this."

"Did you forget how to act, Mamet?"

"What's wrong with you?"

"Do it again."

"Do it again."

"DO IT AGAIN."

Eventually he gave up or got bored. But this lasted for about a half hour. And nobody stopped it. Everyone just stared at their shoes while he screamed at me. Eventually we finished the blocking rehearsal and shot the scene. I finished my day. I walked to my car and called my agents and told them I quit. I was supposed to do four more episodes that season, not including the one I was on, but I told them I didn't care what they had to do, I didn't care if the network sued me, I refused to go back on that set for one more day than I actually had to. I don't remember anything else about the rest of that shoot. I think I've blocked it out.

The show went on to break records for awards and ratings. And it deserved it. It's an incredible piece of television, and I feel insanely honored to have been a part of it. I feel proud of the work I did on that show and I wouldn't take back any of it for a second. It's all a learning experience, right?

I ran into that showrunner at the Emmys a few years later. Both of our shows were nominated. He pretended not to know who I was. They swept the awards that night and part of me resented him for that. But you know, he hasn't really made anything since. And sometimes I think about him sitting in his office alone feeling sad and angry and anxious and wondering if everyone's forgotten him, and for a moment it makes me feel sorry for him, feel compassion for him, hope that his life isn't too bad . . .

But let's be real, only for a moment.

ABSOLUTELY FAAAAAABULOUS

I wasn't allowed to watch TV growing up, which I don't think would have bothered me at all if it weren't for other kids. Standing around at school in the morning while everyone else discussed the previous night's episode of *The Simpsons* and not being able to weigh in about what had happened or even the characters was incredibly isolating. But other than the removal from pop culture, I didn't mind too much. And not having access to general television is what contributed to my knowledge of great TV and film of the past.

My love of old movies started with my grandmother, who probably thought cable was a scam. She got her news from the newspaper and her entertainment from the theater, and if she wanted to watch a film, she had every one she could desire on VHS in a closet off the room that housed her very old, very chunky television. She also had a huge, old, cushioned chair that would envelop me as I allowed myself to be swept away by the brilliant movie stars from yesteryear. That chair is where I fell in love with the Hepburns, Cary Grant, Doris Day, Jimmy Durante, Judy Garland, and the like. I'd cycle through the tapes over and over again. I'd always wanted to be an actress, but I truly think my grandmother's old TV and those VHS tapes sealed the deal for me. I'll never forget the first time I saw *Bringing Up Baby*. I thought Katharine Hepburn was a superhero. And I wanted to be her. I wanted to know how to re-create that magic.

I moved in with my father when I was seventeen, and that's when the second phase of my film and TV education began. My dad didn't have TV either, but I think that's because mostly he believes that everything made after the year 1985 is a piece of shit. In another household without cable I was yet again forced to make do with what was available to me. This is when I discovered Vidiots. Vidiots is a rental spot in Santa Monica that houses pretty much every movie and TV show you could possibly imagine on DVD, VHS, Blu-ray, you name it. My little sister and I would pop over, looking for a movie my dad had recommended, and end up coming home with stacks to watch.

My dad introduced me to Preston Sturges and Powell & Pressburger. He taught me to worship at the altar of Barbara Stanwyck, who, to this day, is my favorite actress to ever grace the silver screen. And he taught me about British television.

Everyone in my family is a diehard fan of British TV. *Fawlty Towers*, *Are You Being Served?*, and of course, the end all be all, *Absolutely Fabulous*. I was OBSESSED with *Ab Fab* (and still am). The explosion of brilliance between those two women on that show never ceases to amaze me. I can watch it on repeat, never getting bored, the jokes never getting old—just forever in love and in awe of what they had created.

One day, after all my friends had gone off to college and I was hustling my ass around LA trying to start a career for myself, the unthinkable happened: I got a call from my agent, who told me that they were making an American pilot of *Ab Fab* for Fox and I had gotten an audition to play Saffron, the daughter.

Now, if you haven't seen this show, just do yourself a favor and watch it. The premise is that Edina and Patsy are two best friends who are, you guessed it, fabulous, moneyed, disastrously drunk pretty much all the time, and constantly getting themselves into and miraculously out of absolute messes. Edina's daughter, Saffron, or Saffy, is the lovable annoying straight man who is constantly trying to get them both in line. She's a total bore as a human and what most would call a party pooper, but she is the grounded foil to the glitter-bomb insanity of Eddy and Patsy, and the show wouldn't be the comedy genius that it is without her. Also, the straight man is often the most fun to play. Getting to be the down note of the melody is hard as fuck, but when you can do it right, it feels like flying.

Never in a million years did I think I would get this part. It was my dream role, and because it was my dream role is precisely why it would never happen. And yet there I was, reading scenes for an audition for that very role, not really allowing myself to entertain the idea but somewhere in the deep hopeful recesses of my mind, a tiny whisper was mouthing, But what if you got it?

I went for the audition. And, shockingly, it went great. And I left and thought, Okay. That was nice. You did a good job. Well done. Now back to normal life.

And then I got a callback. And the whisper in the basement of my brain got a little louder: Okay but WHAT IF you got it?! It was just a callback, so it wasn't like I had an offer or anything. But I went for the callback. And, at the risk of sounding immodest, I slayed it.

Today, it's a bit of a the-rules-are-what-we-make-them situation when it comes to getting a job as an actor. Movie stars do television, the kernels of ideas are pre-optioned to be turned into movie franchises before the podcasts the movies will be based on have even been made, and pretty much every decision is made by an algorithm. But network TV did and does and probably always will have a process one has to go through in order to get a job.

It starts with an initial audition. If you make it through that round, you're on to the callback. Occasionally there will be a few rounds of callbacks with various different people joining, normally starting with producers and then moving onto the director. Sometimes there will be a chemistry read thrown in there somewhere to make sure that you mesh well with the other actors you'll be working with. And then, if you are still alive at this point in the process, you get what's called a test offer, which is like an unofficial job offer that also goes out to anywhere between maybe three to six other girls who are also up for your part. The hardest part about a test offer is that you negotiate your contract beforehand, AS IF the job is already yours. You see how many years you would be filming the show, how much money you'd be making, what a bonus if you win awards would be. You negotiate down to the nitty-gritty of what size trailer you'd have. So the job feels real even though it isn't yet. It's like the love of your life saying, "I'll marry whoever out of the three of you bakes the pie I like most." And so you're left with the pressure of knowing that your dream life is one good pie away. It's a mindfuck.

Eventually I got a test offer for *Ab Fab*. It was the first one I'd ever gotten.

There are two steps to the testing process: the studio and then the network. Like the two final bosses of a video game that you must slay in order to be let into the kingdom of heaven. Which in this case was the Fox lot.

I don't remember much of my studio test other than it was held in a theater on the Sony lot. There must have been forty people sitting in the audience, but they all looked like AI clone versions of the same studio executive. Bland black suits, slicked-back hair, thumbs frantically typing on BlackBerrys (yes, they still had those). Not a single one of them looked up during my audition. The rest of it is a blur. I blacked out. But I do remember the exhaustion I felt as I left, as if I had been squeezing every ounce of my body as hard as I could for hours, and when I finally released it, the fatigue washed over me like a downpour.

I was still semi-starving myself at this point in my life, but the hunger that came over me then was bigger than my body dysmorphia. On the way home, I stopped at a diner and inhaled a double hamburger because I felt if I didn't fuel my body with something primal in that very second I was going to turn to dust.

As I was sitting at the counter, hands covered in ketchup because I'd obviously removed the bun and wrapped my double meat stack in lettuce (how did I ever live life without carbs?), I got the call from my agent that I had made it through to the final round of this godforsaken process, the network test. It was scheduled for that evening on the Fox lot. So I finished my burger, went home, napped, and then made my way to the Thunderdome for the last stand.

We were in one of those old bungalows that they still have on the lot, which I found oddly comforting as opposed to being in some nondescript room on some random level in one of the new buildings. I was still in the same clothes, and as I walked into the waiting room, I wondered if I smelled like hamburger, but it was too late to turn back. There were two other girls in the waiting room, so they had narrowed it down to three of us. The casting director came out and told us the order we'd go in—I was last.

As the first girl disappeared into the room and I heard laughter bubbling up to the ceiling, I realized I didn't feel nervous, I felt numb. The level of want I had for this job was almost too much to comprehend. I had come so far, I was so close I could almost taste it. I couldn't handle the nervousness or the want or the fear because I would have probably wet my pants and then short-circuited if I'd allowed those feelings to course through me. So instead I just stared at my shoes.

And then it was my turn. There were about twenty-five people in the room. I recognized the faces of the casting director, her associate, and Jimmy Burrows, who was directing, but other than that they were all strangers. It was better that way—I could just pretend they weren't there. I'd done the scenes so many times at that point that they were ingrained in me. We did them once.

I remember the laughter—genuine chuckles from the faceless, nameless humans who were in this room to decide my fate. My jury laughed. Jimmy gave me a note and we did it again. After he looked at our casting director and nodded, she walked up to me, put her arms around me, and with a massive smile on her face announced to the room, "Everyone, please meet our Saffron." Everyone in the room stood up and began uproariously clapping and I burst into hysterical sobs.

To this day I don't think I have ever felt such a mixture of joy and relief. At first I thought I was dreaming, but they kept clapping and smiling and congratulating me. I had done it, I had gotten the job. It was one of the best moments of my life. And in many ways it was the beginning of my career.

Making that pilot was some of the most fun I've ever had. The scripts were brilliant, the team was amazing.

Kathryn Hahn played Edina and I fell so in love with that woman. She was pregnant with her first child while we were filming, and her emotions were at an all-time high in a way that made her even more fabulous than when she wasn't busy making a human in her belly. She'd randomly burst out into hysterical sobs at the most hilarious moments, which only endeared her to everyone more. She was so kind and protective of me, and made me feel safe and smart and good at my job. On our show night, when I was on the verge of vomiting I was so nervous, she slid a card under my door that read, "I hope I have a girl, and I hope she is just like you." To this day thinking about that card makes me tear up. I still have it.

Kristen Johnston played Patsy and she was equally as wonderful in her own wild way. When I would get flustered she'd tell me to calm down and take it again. She'd crack the most obscene jokes when tensions got too high, immediately defusing the situation. She was brash and loud and unapologetically herself.

The two of them together were comedy gold. And Jimmy? There are no words. I would have been happy just sitting there and watching but getting to be a part of it was icing on the cake.

The show was a smash. My first entrance, I flubbed my line and then said "Fuck" after I'd biffed it in front of a live studio audience, to which Kristen loudly bellowed, "Don't worry, honey, it's only TV." I went back out, came back in, and it was smooth sailing after that. The week was a dream. The Santa Ana winds were gusting with gale forces and on show night we all took a golf cart over to the commissary to get some dinner. On the way there, sitting on the back of that golf cart trying not to get blown off, a massive gust came through and blew my hair into my face, a few tendrils whipping directly into my eyeball. My eye started watering and I could barely see. The following Monday, I ended up at an eye doctor, who told me I had probably slightly scratched my cornea, but the high I was on that day, that week? I couldn't even feel it.

Sadly, the show biz gods seemed to have other plans in store for me, and right before up-fronts, I got the dreaded call from my agent that *Ab Fab* was not going to be picked up. I was devastated. However, I found comfort in the fact that I had crossed something off of my bucket list that I hadn't even put on it before because the thought of it happening seemed so obscene. I'd played one of the roles that had made me fall in love with television and with comedy. And even though it pains me to say this because my self-deprecating brain tells me I'll be struck down with a lightning bolt for so much as thinking it . . . I'd played it well and I was proud of that.

Two years later I got *Girls*. Which I couldn't have done if *Ab Fab* had been picked up. I don't know what I believe in—free will, a divine plan, fate, etc.—but in moments like that, sometimes it's nice for a little while to believe that everything happens for a reason.

And I kind of like to think that playing Saffy, even for that brief moment, in a way prepped me for playing Shosh. They couldn't be more different if they tried, but they were both the straight man. And sometimes if I'm looking for a chuckle I imagine them at some fancy New York bar, having hilariously awkward and wonderfully uncomfortable drinks together. Saffron rolling her eyes in frustration while Shosh tries to get her to answer which *Sex and the City* character she thinks she is, which, obviously? Miranda.

THE PUMPKINS FROZE

To me, the entertainment industry has always been a bit like a problematic boyfriend I just can't give up. The kind where your friends say, Dude, why are you still with that guy? He treats you like shit, he takes you for granted, and the sex isn't even that great. To which I respond, I can't help myself, I love him.

I didn't have an easy time starting out. But, like a bad relationship, I just kept coming back for more. My dad used to say to me it isn't about talent, it's about persistence. He'd tell me that every time a door was shut in my face, I just had to wait outside of it until someone opened it back up. And eventually they'd get so fucking sick of me standing outside of their door that they'd let me in.

Given the fact that I've now had my fair share of success in this industry, I guess this worked. It isn't exactly the nicest thing to think, that you annoyed everyone to a point that they gave in rather than deal with your nagging, but I guess I'll take it.

The nicer theory, of course, is that they finally recognized my talent and gave me a shot. Although that theory requires me to think I have talent, and let's be real, I'm an actor, obviously my self-worth is lacking.

But whatever the reason, I kept at it, and eventually the tides began to turn. Jobs popped up here and there until one day I booked the lead in a movie.

It was an indie film. The premise was described to me as *Sabrina the*

Teenage Witch meets *Divine Secrets of the Ya-Ya Sisterhood*. Looking back I wonder how I ever thought this would be a good idea, but I was young and desperate, so my judgment was somewhat skewed.

The movie shot in upstate New York, so I packed up my things and headed across the country.

The shoot was a disaster from day one. I spent most of the film in a dress made out of literal trash bags, which in hindsight was a glaring omen. The director, who had halted auditions after she had seen mine, claiming that I was exactly what she had been looking for, swiftly developed an unnerving dislike for me. She kept asking me to do things that were so counter to who I was that I honestly began to wonder if they had quite literally cast the wrong girl.

Besides her desire to morph me into someone I wasn't, she was just generally awful. She was mean to the crew, who a week into the shoot had already started calling her "the dragon lady" for her seething temper. She and the director of photography (the human in charge of the camera) argued like a married couple on meth. She had no idea what she was doing. We never finished what had been scheduled to be shot on any given day because the shoot overall was such a mess. The woman playing my mother was, to put it nicely, a loose cannon. And to top it all off, we were cheating the coldest October on record for what was meant to be a balmy early September. There were no pumpkins to be had for Halloween that year because the crops had all died from a record-breaking early frost.

I was in every scene of the movie except one. And ninety-five percent of the film was shot either at exterior locations or inside this house that had no electricity or running water. I swear to this day it was colder in that house than it was outside. Needless to say, I was freezing all the time. But though this shoot was memorable for many reasons, the worst memory is when I got pneumonia.

It was a night shoot. We started filming around midnight in the middle of the woods. On this night in particular I was meant to have been in a car accident, and we were going to show me slowly, magically healing myself. In order to get this shot I had to lie on the frozen forest floor for hours. I was wearing ripped tights and a T-shirt dress. I remember it was so cold that we had to keep resetting the shot because my body was uncontrollably shaking. The director and the director of photography couldn't agree on the shot, and in order to get what we needed for the special effects that would be added in postproduction, I had to remain perfectly still. But my body kept convulsing from the cold, so we had to keep restarting. I lay there for hours, the frozen air and ground mixing together, seeping their way into my bones. We shot until the sun came up.

By that point, everything was numb. I couldn't even feel the cold anymore. I remember getting back to my tiny apartment and taking a bath. The water was so hot I could see it scalding my skin but I couldn't feel it. That was the night I got pneumonia.

It came on hard and fast. The cough is the main thing I remember: I would cough so hard I'd throw up. I'd feel fluid rattling in my lungs. But we were on a tight budget and an even tighter schedule. Shooting six-day weeks with only Sundays off, there was no time to go to the doctor. So they brought one to me.

"Doctor" is a generous word for the woman who arrived on set. I'd call her more of a medicine woman with questionable morals, given that I am fully convinced the producers paid her to improperly diagnose me so I could continue working. I was too young to know better at this point, and I had been brought up to believe doctors. So when she told me I had a run-of-the-mill cold and prescribed hot water with lemon and honey and echinacea, I did as I was told. I continued working sixteen-to-eighteen-hour days in my trash-bag dress outside in the pumpkin-killing cold while my pneumonia got worse and worse.

Somewhere among all of this insanity I got an audition for a TV pilot. I remember my agent calling me and saying that he thought this one was special. I was sent a link to the writer's film, which had just swept the festival circuit, along with four pages of sides for the audition. (Sides, for those who don't know, are what we call the pages of dialogue for the scenes we are sent when we have an audition. In this case it was a single scene between the character I was auditioning for and another woman, her cousin.)

The film stood up to every ounce of hype. The sides were good. Really good. But that's all I got. Four pages and a few sentences of a character description. By this point, the pneumonia had created a film of depression around me. I had become convinced this movie, if we ever finished it and if anyone ever saw it, would ruin my career that had seemingly just begun. So while the dream of another job after this disastrous one was a beacon of hope, at that point, I was too sick to care.

I needed someone to make the tape with me. But that weekend, the entire crew, beginning to buck against the prison of our calamitous shoot, had all escaped to the city. The only person left was our devout Christian production assistant. I somehow convinced her to skip church with her husband and newborn to help me tape my television audition.

Our "production office" was in an abandoned barn with unreliable Wi-Fi. I was too ill to care about anything like makeup or lighting or brushing my hair, so I rolled out of bed, splashed water on my face, threw my greasy hair up into a bun, and pulled on an oversized sweater that I had stolen from my father.

I did a single take of the audition. It was all I had in me. And then I spent the next five hours trying to get the tape to send. I am terrible with technology. I am convinced it knows this and fucks with me just for fun. But anything tech-related never ends well for me. After hour three of being told "Your file is too large to send" and "Wi-Fi con-nection unstable," I called my agent and told him I was giving up, but he begged me to keep trying. Eventually, somehow, I sent it off, went back to my apartment, and passed out.

A week went by. I didn't hear anything, which isn't abnormal. Sometimes you never hear a thing beyond the fact that they received your tape. Sometimes you don't even get that.

I was in the costume trailer being ironed into my trash-bag dress when my agent called.

"You got the job," he said.

"What job?"

"The one you taped for last week."

"Wait, I GOT that?"

"Yes, you got it.

"Wait, are you sure?"

We went around in circles like this for a while. Maybe it was the fluid in my lungs, but I just couldn't wrap my head around the fact that they had liked my pneumonia-haze, dirty-hair tape. I've since come to believe that sometimes when it comes to acting, the best work is born when you literally aren't able to think about it too much. On that Sunday afternoon in an abandoned barn with a sweet Christian PA, I was far too sick and exhausted to do anything but trust my instincts and be unabashedly myself. When I read the sides I remember thinking, I feel like I might know exactly who this girl is. I guess the creative powers that be had agreed.

The role was just a guest star in the pilot. They were shooting the pilot first; the show hadn't been picked up to series yet. The following Monday I had off, and it just so happened that was the day they were having a table read for the pilot in Manhattan. So I slogged through another grueling week on that miserable film shoot. Another week of vicious rattling coughs, eighteen-hour days in the freezing cold, bull-shit herbal remedies prescribed by the "doctor," and verbal abuse from our director, who had taken to yelling things at me like, "Why can't you just be what I want?!"

By the time Sunday rolled around, I was a shell of myself. I looked like shit, I sounded like shit, I felt like shit.

The table read was in the morning, so I traveled in by bus on Sunday and stayed with a friend of mine. On the way from the bus station to her apartment, I stopped to load up on cold medication. I got Gatorade and cough drops, and on my way to the register I grabbed NyQuil. I needed to be well rested for the next day, so I wanted something to knock me out so I wouldn't cough all night. I couldn't remember the last time I'd taken NyQuil, but everyone swears by it, right, so I figured it was a safe bet.

I got to my friend's apartment, took a shower, got into my pajamas, popped two NyQuil capsules, and went to bed.

The following day is hazy at best. I remember getting in the car that had been sent to pick me up. I do not remember waking up or getting dressed or having coffee. I was wearing a blue wool hooded cloak that I'd bought in a thrift store in Ventura with the same oversized sweater I'd been wearing in my audition, skinny jeans, and knee-high vintage Robin Hood boots. I don't remember putting one item of this clothing on. It was raining, I remember that.

When I walked onto the stage at Silvercup Studios, I was wet. And when I get sick or overtired, I get dark red circles under my eyes. Looking back on my appearance—wet, spacey, sickly red undereye circles—I think I must have looked like an addict. I walked onto the stage where a long table and chairs were set up with more folding chairs facing the table for the "audience." I was introduced to Judd

Apatow and Lena Dunham and shook their hands. I sat down at the table.

And then I do not remember a single thing until I woke up on the floor of my friend's apartment hours later drenched in sweat. I gasped for air, panic coursing through my veins. I tried to place myself, tried to grasp for context. Where had I just been, what had just happened. I replayed the day in my brain. But after I got to sitting down at the table, the tape went blank and I remembered nothing, except a vague recollection that wafted in and out like a bad recording.

I could see myself at the table, the table read under way, and suddenly, in this clouded half memory, I threw up all over the table. We're talking constant projectile vomit. Everywhere. And then, the tape goes blank and I have nothing again until I woke up on the floor.

I called my agent, hysterical. I couldn't stop crying, convinced that I had not only royally biffed this opportunity but that I had ruined any chance at a future career.

"You threw up?!"

"I don't know. I THINK I did? I can't remember anything but I think I may have thrown up in the middle of the table read."

"Okay, okay, let me call them. Sit tight, it's gonna be okay."

I didn't hear from him for a week. In the meantime, my imagination ran wild. It went down back roads and dark alleys that led me to conclusions like, They're going to sue you for breach of contract and destruction of studio property. They're going to send out a memo to all of HBO saying that you're an irresponsible meth addict and that nobody should hire you ever again. You're going to have to move to Canada because you won't even be able to get a job at McDonald's. You're gonna go to jail because somehow what you did must be illegal.

I spun and I spun until I couldn't spin anymore and I ended up back at, You're getting fired. Which in and of itself was horrible. This hadn't been my fault. I was being run ragged on a job I hated that had such horrific working conditions I had gotten horribly ill. And in an attempt to be responsible and get a good night sleep I had ended up accidentally overdrugging and making a fool of myself. I was heartbroken and I was pissed.

A week to the day after the table read, I was back on the movie set. Again, in the costume truck. Again, being ironed into my trash-bag dress.

My phone rang. It was my agent.

"They want to make you a series regular," he said.

"Who does?"

"The show. The reason they haven't gotten back to me is they were amending your contract. They want to change your character from a guest star to a series regular."

"I don't understand," I said. "I threw up on the table. I thought I was fired?"

"Apparently you didn't. And apparently you're not. They loved what you did so much that they want to change it from three girls to four. You are the fourth."

"Okay," I said, still having trouble processing.

"I guess you should take NyQuil more often! The pilot shoots in November. I'll call you back with details once we have them."

I stood in the wardrobe trailer, numb. I had been so convinced that my career was over that this turn of events was hard to wrap my head around. But now that I think back on it, I wonder if I do in fact have NyQuil to thank for the biggest break of my career. With my nerves and a large portion of my brain capacity kept at bay by a cough suppressant, there was no room for me to overthink anything in that table read. All I could be was myself.

We shot the pilot that November as planned. The show got picked up to series and we began shooting the following spring. I moved from LA to New York to start my new life. I never saw that movie and I never heard from that director ever again. I spent the next seven years shooting the TV show playing what was and will likely always be my favorite part I've ever played. That show, *Girls*, changed my career and my life.

I often wonder if I would have gotten that job without the pneumonia or the NyQuil. We will never know. I was never nominated for anything for that show, but when I would daydream about winning an Emmy, I always planned to thank NyQuil in my acceptance speech. Credit where credit is due, ya know?

Olympia Dukakis had played my grandmother in that horrific film. I adored her from the moment I saw her. The first night we met at a cast dinner, she arrived fantastically late, sat down, grabbed the waiter literally by his tie, and said, "Tequila, on the rocks with four Equals and a lime." She peed in a bucket one day on set because the producers wouldn't let her walk back to her trailer. "Well then get me a bucket. I'm not holding this in for another take!" she said. She was a tornado and I was in awe of her.

I had the privilege of working with her again years later. The first day I saw her on set, she walked up to me and said, "That movie was a piece of shit, huh?!"

It was. That film shoot was one of the worst experiences of my life. But I also have it to thank for so much. The same way you learn from horrible relationships, you can learn from disastrous jobs what you want *and* what you don't want. On that shoot, I learned creative ways to stay warm, that pneumonia is really only cured with heavy-duty antibiotics and not manuka honey, that you shouldn't take Ny-Quil the night before you have to be a functioning professional (or maybe you should?), and that sometimes, against all odds, things happen exactly how they're supposed to.

Years later, when looking for a photo of something, my husband stumbled upon the *Girls* audition tape hiding within the bowels of my computer. I hadn't seen the tape since I'd made it all those years ago. But there I was, snot-nosed and dirty-haired in my father's oversized sweater. Sitting on a chair in that slapdash "office" in an abandoned barn. I'm holding my sides looking just off camera, and sitting on a shelf right behind me, miraculously, is a pumpkin.

Part 3

Astronomical Twilight

AMOUR

We remember it differently.

As memories go, that's bound to happen.

He claims he was already there. Perhaps he was. It could be that my mind has embellished or manipulated the memory to tell a better story. Not on purpose of course but minds are clever like that.

So he claims he was already there, but I remember it differently.

I was nervous. I was debilitatingly nervous. I'm a nervous person in general, but not as much about work. For some reason when it comes to work, I've always had some semblance of calm. Maybe I'm just kidding myself and it's a protective function, but I know my lines, I show up on time, I'm always game and ready. I come prepared.

But this day, this day I was fucking nervous.

While years of Ambien addiction and pill popping and starvation have made my mind a bit muddy at times, for the most part I remember our first meeting pretty clearly, minus details like what I was wearing. (I'm sure it was some version of my body-shrouding wardrobe at the time: jeans, boots, a massively oversized sweater I found at a thrift store and probably once belonged to a large elderly man.) I was the only non-theater actress in the play. And I was playing the lead—a part I had fought tooth and nail to get.

Initially, they hadn't let me read for it. They kept asking me to read for the sister role. The sister role was bubbly and brash and had all the one-liners. She was funny; she was the comedic relief. But I didn't want to do that this time. I knew I was capable of playing the flip side, and I wanted to prove to myself and everyone else that I could do it. So I kept fighting. And then randomly, a girlfriend of mine asked me to do a favor for a friend of hers—to be in their music video. It was an up-and-coming indie band and she was supposed to do it for them but had gotten stuck in LA. Would I do a one-night shoot on a Saturday as a favor for a friend of a friend? Sure, why not.

The song was dark. A breakup song. And in the video, the girl innocently offers to cook the man who has just broken up with her one last meal. To his surprise she's peppered it with tiny shards of glass, and the music video ends with her exuberantly watching as he coughs up blood until he bleeds out and dies . . . light stuff.

The playwright, who had thought I couldn't play dark and so wouldn't let me audition for the lead role, randomly happened to see the music video and changed his mind. He finally let me read, and I got the part.

I'd never done a play before. And everyone in the cast were theater actors—real actors, in my mind. I worried that they thought I was a stupid, vapid TV-acting bimbo and hated me. So I was nervous. You get it.

I walked into the rehearsal space and said hi to everyone in a bit of a daze—excited and pounding with adrenaline and imposter syndrome, assuming that at any moment someone would come in with a clipboard and look at me and whisper to the director, who would come up to me and explain that they'd made a mistake and I wasn't actually playing the lead, I was playing the couch instead. But that didn't happen. Instead, everyone shook my hand excitedly and introduced themselves warmly and nobody seemed to have a clipboard at all. At least not that I could see.

And then I heard someone say, "Oh hey, Evan, you can have a seat anywhere."

This is where our memories diverge. Because he claims he was already there, that he never would have been the last to arrive. But we'll go with my version for this story . . .

So I heard someone greet him and I turned around and there he was. Standing right in front of me. And my insides left my body. Someone introduced me and Evan put out his hand for me to shake. I'm assuming I formed words of some sort, because he's never claimed I didn't, but I don't recall speaking, I just remember shaking his hand. Touching him for the first time. My skin to his. Even just a tiny handshake and electricity shot through my entire body. The age-old cliché, I lived it. And I could have sworn on our dog's life that I said "FUCK" out loud, but that would be part of his story, and it isn't, so I guess I didn't. But I certainly said it in my head.

The rest of the day is a blur to me. I know we read the play through a number of times. Table work, as they call it in the theater. I don't remember any of it. I just remember that first moment. And his eyes. They're the kind you can't quite name the color of. They're piercing and kind and they looked right through me.

Two days before we met, I had sworn off men. I'd just gone through a slew of relationships—all varying lengths and levels of seriousness, but relationships nonetheless. One was an on-again, off-again alcoholic who nearly convinced me to marry him. That one led into a fast and furious love affair with a single dad living in a different state, finishing his PhD. I'd fly back and forth between New York and his hometown to visit him and his daughter until it became clear to me that he thought having a relationship meant he was a bad dad. So that petered out. And then I got played by a grade-A player I didn't even want to date in the first place but who somehow hoodwinked me into falling for him. He played me like a goddamn fiddle after I'd given him my favorite copy of *The Godfather*—a thrift store find I knew I wasn't getting back.

After that string of gentlemen, I had decided to just call it. I was done being disappointed. I had always yearned for a partner—for my partner—so badly. I can be a bit of a loner, an outlier, but ever since I was little I knew there was another oddly shaped puzzle piece out there waiting to be clicked into place with me. Maybe that sounds overly romantic or soapy, and it probably is, but I'd always felt it, deep in my core. But after so many failed attempts I gave it up—the search, the trying. I hated dating. What other people found fun I found exhausting and depressing, and honestly, I'd rather be home reading a good book. So I decided if I was gonna be alone, I may as well be happy and not searching for something that didn't exist. I had a great job that I loved, I had great friends. I figured maybe I'd end up with cats (even though I hate cats) but at least I'd be fulfilled in these other ways. And without dating, I'd have all this free time to devote to bettering myself as a human! I could learn a language, I could learn two languages, I could take an art class, I could finally learn how to ride a motorcycle! Or take up needlepoint. Or learn how to needlepoint motorcycles! The options were endless. I was honestly excited about this new life path. Thus Single Zosia was born.

Her existence lasted two days.

I hate the cliché that things come when you least expect them. Or when you finally let go and stop trying to find them. But clichés are usually clichés for a reason, which is annoying but true. So I gave it up. I let go, I turned in my punch card, threw away the key, and whatever other classic terminology you want to fill in here, and then into my life he walked.

Literally, he walked into my life.

The first week rehearsing was a little bit tough because on day two of rehearsal in our break room I overhead him telling another castmate about a girl who I assumed was his girlfriend. He talked about what an angel she was and how she was working for Teach for America and all she wanted to do was give back and how basically she was perfect in every way, and all I could think was, Super, I'm fucked, he's dating Mother Teresa. What am I gonna do—be a home-wrecker for a saint?! Thankfully, I soon discovered the woman he'd been describing was his roommate, and with some additional sleuthing, I figured out that he was in fact single.

Perfect, right?

Not exactly.

Here's something you should know about me: I have ZERO game. This isn't me being modest. I truly do not have a slick bone in my body. Zero, zilch, nothing. Do not ask me for dating advice because I will without fail tell you the wrong thing to do and it won't be cool or clever or even cute.

So instead of being chill and asking him out or whatever someone with game does, I decided to use every single one of the tickets I had for my upcoming *Girls* premiere for every single member of the play, just so I could invite Evan.

I had of course convinced myself he wasn't going to come. And then I realized what a sociopath I was being. How could I feel this intensely about a guy I barely even knew? And was I going to ruin this stunning Givenchy dress that I needed two people to help me get into because it was so tight by vomiting on it from nerves? No, I wasn't. But I wanted him to come so badly. I wanted him to come like a kid wants a puppy for Christmas.

And look—it may not have been sly, but it worked. He came! Along with the other fifteen members of our cast and crew or however many there were. And it was an amazing night. When I saw his face among the crowd, it was like a sunflower had bloomed inside my chest and then exploded with Valium sparkles throughout my body. I don't remember the screening. I don't remember getting to the party. But once I was there, I remember it like a favorite film I've watched over and over and over again. We found each other immediately. We worked the room like we were already a couple. He kept his hand on the small of my back. Not in a possessive way, just in a kind and sexy, I'm-right-here-and-you-look-beautiful-and-I-like-touching-you way. The night went by in a finger snap in my memory, like a sped-up record with flashes of light and sound and joy interspersed.

And then Evan said ever so coolly that he'd had the most amazing time but he had to go. Unlike me, Evan has game. If I am a broken pogo stick, he is a race car. The man oozes game. So of course he was going to come, slay, and then leave before things got messy or complicated.

I knew we'd see each other the following day at rehearsal, but the anxiety in me needed to put a stamp on this, needed to know there was more. And so before he left, I came out with the only thing I could think of in my zero-game mind. I asked him if he wanted to run lines sometime.

Here's the reason why this is so pathetic: Evan is ever the professional and likes being off book (i.e., not reading from the script) from the jump so he isn't wedded to trying to remember his lines. He has the freedom to play if he knows them already. I was already off book because I was so insanely nervous the rest of the cast wouldn't think I was the real deal, so I had overprepared and walked into day one of rehearsal already knowing every single one of my lines. And we both knew that the other one already knew all of their lines. So my "let's run lines sometime" suggestion was obviously me asking him to hang out without asking him to hang out because I didn't have the balls to just ask him to hang out.

He said yes, because he's a nice guy.

And a few nights later we got together to "run lines." We had our scripts open and we may have run a single scene once, but that was about it. Instead, we sat on the floor of my apartment and talked about everything. I remember thinking, I want to spend every moment with this human. I felt high. Like I could float. Like I'd injected my veins with helium.

The next day at rehearsal, we ran into each other in the hall and he said what a nice time he'd had. And I said something like, "Yeah we should run lines again sometime." And he said, "Or not," and I died inside.

Because OBVIOUSLY, I thought, Ohhhh right of course, OF COURSE this handsome, talented, funny, smart, kind, sexy human isn't into me. Last night was a fluke. Last night he was just being nice. And now he's just being honest; you asked if he wanted to do it again and he's just being forthright and saying, Yeah, I'm not gonna string you along, no thanks, it was nice, but I'll be going now.

Now, in retrospect, I can see that obviously what he meant by "or not run lines" was "do something else."

But again, being that I'm an anxiety junkie who loves to spiral out in my brain about things that aren't based in reality, that's what I did. For the rest of rehearsal I had an internal meltdown about how the man I thought I could possibly fall in love with had just full-blown dismissed me and now I had to go through an entire run of a play pining for him.

At the end of the day, he asked when we were hanging out again. And the anxiety melted like the polar ice caps.

He came over a few nights later. He had told me he was going to see the movie *Amour* and asked me if I wanted to come. Again, being an idiot, I assumed it was a pity invite and he really wanted to see the movie alone but felt bad not inviting me, so I told him, "No, that's okay, I'll wait here for you, and just come over when the movie ends." What a ding-dong. (Sometimes I wonder what I could do with the amount of brain power my anxiety sucks up. I could probably power a fleet of electric vehicles. I could probably cure cancer. Or like at least be slightly less haunted and tortured in my day-to-day life.)

He came over after the movie. Now, if you haven't seen it, this movie is about true, undying, everlasting love of beyond epic proportions. It is the kind of movie that plays your heartstrings like they were the entire string section of the Philharmonic. It is human and beautiful and it will fuck you up.

When Evan showed up, he was gushing about how emotional the movie was and how he wanted to find a person to love like that, and on and on [insert emotional tidal wave here]. I sat on the floor staring at him sitting in the single chair I had in my apartment and I just thought, Please for the love of all things holy let me be that person.

For the rest of the night, we talked about everything and nothing. Eventually he gave me the most beautiful speech about how he knew this play meant so much to both of us and that we're both professionals and we'd never do anything that would get in the way of our work, but that he thought I was amazing and he wasn't going anywhere and that if we weren't working together he would kiss me and that we could always see what happens after the play.

And then he kissed me and we ferociously made out on my apartment floor.

Man's. Got. Game.

We dated secretly for the rest of the play until we finally got caught—ten days before closing. Our Saturday matinee schedule was psychotic, and we thought we had a three o'clock matinee but we actually had a two o'clock matinee. My apartment building was a weird black hole for cell service, and at 1:48, after just having gotten out of a very long shower (ahem), we both looked at our phones and had twenty missed calls each from producers, stage manager, director, castmates.

We were onstage by 2:08, but showing up that late together and both sporting wet hair kind of gave us away. We said we'd been at lunch . . . in the rain.

So that's how it began. Thirteen years later and those eyes still slay me every time I look into them. I don't know if we'll ever agree on how it began, but that doesn't really matter now, does it?

MIRROR MIRROR

There was a freedom to it like I had never known. One I didn't expect. It didn't set in right away. It took a while to build up in my system and truly take hold. But once it did it's what I imagine enlightenment feels like. A true and utter disembodiment.

I've spent my entire life feeling like a captive inside my own skin. I used to describe it when I was younger, or I guess I still do, as feeling like I'm covered in a film. As if the layers of fat I feel all over me are a thick suit I want to rip off every second of every day. I feel suffocated by and disgusted with and disconnected from myself. I read a story once about how a girl cut her belly fat off with a butcher knife. Just chopped it off. And no part of me was shocked. I understood. I still understand why she did it, what drove her to such an extreme action. Hatred is a powerful emotion.

Intellectually, I've always understood my triggers. Whenever I have to have my photo taken. At work, if I'm wearing something tight or revealing or that I don't feel comfortable in. Events where I'm surrounded by beautiful skinny people, fittings, or trying on clothes in general. Wearing a bathing suit. The usual things that plague most women walking on the earth.

But I never thought about mirrors. They're such a part of our lives. They're everywhere. They just exist like sinks or the news. So the idea of removing them and what that could do had never occurred to me.

But then my husband and I went on the road. We had always

wanted to drive cross-country in an RV but had never had the chance. And then we found out that a television show I was in was premiering at the San Francisco film festival. Neither of us were working at the time, so we thought, No time like the present. Within a day Evan had planned out the entire trip. We rented an RV and started the drive with our dog, Moose, from New York to San Francisco.

We'd drive for long stretches. Sometimes seven, eight, nine hours in a day. Sometimes through endless stretches of terrain where we were the only vehicle on the road and the road went for longer than our brains could compute. Desert or trees or just land sandwiching us, and going, going, going. Sometimes cows, sometimes horses, but normally just nothingness.

There was one mirror, if you can even call it that, in the RV. It was in the bathroom and was about five by seven inches. You could pretty much see enough of your face to not get toothpaste in your hair and that was about it.

We'd drive and we'd talk and we'd snuggle Moose. I'd make us sandwiches while he drove. I'd read. We'd listen to music and podcasts. We'd make up songs. When we got to our campsite we'd set up shop and take Moose for a run to get out her wiggles. And then we'd make dinner. Good food but always simple. The less cleanup the better. And dinner was always just right and just in the nick of time. After, we'd clean and get into bed and sometimes read but normally be too tired. And we'd have cookies and milk and then fall asleep.

The days began to string together and my eating became more primal. I ate because my body needed fuel. I didn't think about calories or carbs or how much. I ate when I was hungry and until I was full. And being in our little portable unit moving as a bubble out in the wilds of the country, I didn't really care. There wasn't anything around to remind me to.

One month. That's all it took. One month away from mirrors. One month away from my industry and my triggers and the values that our world has placed upon us. One single month and I was free. It felt like getting clean. I suppose that's exactly what it was. I found myself feeling my body, its real size and shape, for the first time I could remember. I actually felt myself. Not a heavy fat suit covering my skin, not a prisoner trapped inside of myself, not hatred or wishing I had the guts to cut off my stomach fat like that other girl had. I just felt myself. And, much to my surprise, it felt good. I liked what I felt. I don't even know how to fully describe the freedom, how to put it into words. The simplest way is that it was like wearing chains on my wrists my entire life and then finally having them taken off.

And then I came back to New York.

Walking out my door and onto the street and into the subway, I could hear it. The voice in my head, that evil whisper. It snapped into me like a rubber band. Every time I passed a beautiful girl: She's skinnier than you. Every time I caught my reflection in a store window: You need to lose five pounds.

It was like a speaker inside my brain when I stepped off the elevator into the offices of the couture brand that was fitting me for their dinner that night. I ran directly into a model who was six-foot-who-knows, the kind of beautiful that makes you stare, the size of a toothpick, the size I have yearned my entire life to be. She was sick. I heard her apologizing to the girls from the brand about her cold. Even snot-nosed and coughing, she was a fucking mermaid.

She was skinny.

That word, that aspirational word.

I walked into the fitting and pulled a dress off the rack of clothes I was given to choose from, and the girl helping me said, "Oh, that dress is very small."

In that moment my freedom disappeared. I crawled back inside myself. I didn't cry during my fitting, but I wanted to. I felt like I had gained ten pounds in five minutes—huge and hideous.

That day was the beginning of a slew of days that continued to not be great.

Once dysmorphia catches hold, it's nearly impossible to kick because everything you think you see corroborates its "reality."

The other day, I ran into someone I hadn't seen in a while, and they told me I looked "great, really healthy." I wanted to crawl in a hole and die. In my mind, they might as well have said, Wow, you got fat since I last saw you.

So what now? How do I pull off the dysmorphic glasses for good? How do I re-create and hold on to the freedom that I found while living on the road?

I don't yet know the answer to that. But I certainly am going to try to find it, and I sincerely hope I do. Because I've tasted freedom and it's as sweet as they say.

SKINNY MAMA

We can't let you into the room unless Mr. Jonigkeit is here."
I'm standing in the middle of a hotel lobby in Times Square, which already is making my skin hot, and all I can think is, Don't Cry. Don't. Fucking. Cry. Don't you dare fucking cry in front of all of these tourists holding their venti lattes in their I LOVE NEW YORK bedazzled hats just waiting for something to tell their relatives at home about.

And this is all your fault, you fucking bitch. No, not the desk clerk. She didn't do anything wrong, she's just doing her job. No, it's you in your white coat and your credentials—this breakdown is on you.

I'm standing in the lobby ready to fall apart because of you, a doctor. A doctor who should have known better. Honestly, it's shocking to me that you don't, but the saddest part is that I think you were telling me what you thought I wanted to hear. I think you were trying to be helpful. How many women have taken your advice and what horrendous path did that send them down?

All I want in the entire world is to check into this Midtown hotel room and cry out the sobs that I can feel building up inside me. I want to sit on the cold floor of the sure-to-be-windowless bathroom and let salty snot drip out of my nose in private.

But the front desk won't let me check in. Because my husband isn't there and he booked the room.

"We have the same last name," I say.

The front desk woman seems deeply uninterested in my plight and also unwavering in her interpretation of "the rules."

"Sorry," she says, "but you're not on the reservation."

So I call my husband, and just the sound of his voice on the other end of the phone makes my voice catch.

"I need you to put my name on the reservation so I can check in. They won't let me check in."

He does what the concierge asks, and as she processes the check-in and hands over the key, an overly aggressive bitch nearby asks, "Are you satisfied now?"

I look to my left, wondering who's growling. And then I realize it's me. Those words came out of my mouth. Who the fuck am I right now? The front desk girl looks exhausted and annoyed and a little bit hurt. And she should be. She has every right to be. It isn't her fault. It really isn't anyone's fault but yours, doctor lady . . .

I'm in the hotel room, looking out onto the New York skyline when my husband calls back to make sure I've gotten in okay. That's when the dam breaks. The sobs come in upsettingly large waves.

I've tried to tease out what exactly it is that you made me feel. I think "confusion" is the word I've landed on. And also just incredible sadness.

I think about those three crystal butterflies that I complimented when I first sat down in your office. I couldn't stop looking at them. And now I can't stop thinking about how I have a similar one sitting on a bookshelf in our living room and now I want to go home and break it into a thousand pieces. Even though it was a gift from a dear friend and it would break his heart. But honestly, owning anything that you also have, that you also cherish, makes me feel like something must be wrong in the universe.

"You're going to have to be incredibly calorie conscious during your pregnancy."

The words fell out of your mouth like you'd said them a thousand times before. Like you'd just said, Take Tums for heartburn, or, If you're constipated, drink more water. You said it like it was a fact. You said it unprompted and apropos of nothing.

I don't have a child. I have not had a child yet. But I came to you to talk about having one. I came to you, as an apprentice does to an expert, to ask all my initial questions, to garner some knowledge, to be put at ease about all of the unknowns that were overwhelming me:

Do I have to go off my antidepressant?

Will I be able to take Advil if I get a headache?

What does genetic testing involve?

How soon will I know if I'm barren or not?

I've been on my birth control since I was seventeen. What will happen when I stop taking it?

I asked about medications I could take or could not take, about postpartum depression, about infant mortality rates.

I did not, in any possible way, ask about weight.

Now, have I thought about it? Endlessly. As a recovering anorexic, the concept of weight and pregnancy is something I have spent more time thinking about than I would care to admit.

But I did not ask YOU about it.

And still, you felt the need to tell me about it.

And not in a doctor-sharing-information-with-a-patient kind of way. You assumed I felt a certain way about it and you offered your unsolicited advice about how I should tackle the pregnancy weight gain beast.

You began listing a number of your famous clients and what you'd done for them. You told me how quickly they bounced back, snatched and bikini ready. You talked to me like a colleague, like you KNOW, like we're colluding.

"I know how quickly you have to be back to fighting shape and I can get you there. You just have to follow my instructions to a T. And look, will you look acceptable in a bikini right away? No. But you'll be able to rock a Tom Ford suit on a red carpet and have everyone wonder how you just gave birth."

You kept using the word "acceptable" as if by not following this noxious plan of yours I won't be acceptable. Forgotten and rejected by society, a troll, an outcast. What a way to think of a pregnant woman or any woman at all.

"I have my girls start out with a small nonfat yogurt for breakfast. Then I normally recommend a handful, about twelve, raw almonds as a snack. For lunch I suggest a light protein, no more than four ounces, with a vegetable. If you REALLY need a snack in the afternoon, I suggest a fruit low on the glycemic index, like half a peach. And then for dinner I always recommend fish and a steamed vegetable."

There wasn't so much as an allusion to a carbohydrate. Or a fat. Or, god fucking forbid, sugar. That is, if we aren't counting the fucking half a peach.

All I could think is that what you listed was probably half of what I eat currently. And yet somehow you're expecting me to eat that while I'm literally building another human inside of my abdomen? I go to a hard Pilates class, and I need a large sandwich and an iced latte afterward in order to not pass out from hunger. I can't imagine how ravenous I'm going to be when there's a parasite inside me stealing the majority of my nutrients. But you want me to eat twelve almonds to tide me over between actual meals?

"I tell my girls they can get away with twenty pounds of weight gain total. That includes the baby, of course. So we're talking about fourteen pounds. Totally doable. Honestly, anyone who gains more than that is just lazy. You shouldn't gain any in your first trimester. Second trimester is where most of the weight gain occurs, but third trimester is really just maintenance. And then obviously workouts. You'll need to really push there. Most of my girls who want to look acceptable [there's that fucking word again] quickly post-pregnancy double up. A back-to-back yoga class or a spin class and pilates. There's really no excuse for not working out properly. You'll need to be burning a lot more if you don't want to pack on the pounds."

You told me how some of "your girls" had gotten away without even so much as looking pregnant until month eight. You said it with such pride and you were clearly expecting me to gasp with delight at all the information you were offering me. You didn't so much as notice that I was staring at you, slack-jawed in horror, trying not to throw up on your overpriced carpet from sheer disgust.

You gave me a starvation diet and told me that I should follow it during pregnancy so I wouldn't become a fat, hideous, ostracized cow.

I'm already scared of pregnancy and motherhood. And I came to you in the hopes you could assuage some of my fears. In the hope you could give me facts and information, to armor me. Instead, you ripped a gaping hole in my insecurities and filled it with utter dread.

I wonder about all the other women who have come to you with the same anxieties and concerns. How they cracked themselves open at your feet asking for guidance and comfort. And how you, in return, handed them a diet.

You just kept talking. You didn't seem to care that I hadn't reacted or responded to anything you'd said. This was a TED Talk, not a conversation.

You told me that with this "healthy eating regimen," my baby would probably only be in the fortieth percentile in terms of weight and height, but that's okay, you said. Smaller babies are better for your vagina, you said. Smaller babies are cuter, you said. And there are always human growth hormones if you want them to be taller later on.

You spewed this information like a guru who has it all figured out. What is the meaning of life? In your professional medical opinion, to be skinny.

And look, for many years I felt the same way. I lived by the same rules. I, in fact, DID eat twelve almonds as not a snack but an entire meal some days. Our society still abides by the decree that nothing is more important or more powerful than being thin. And I am sure women come to you asking for all these secrets you are currently hurling at me. They want to know how to look six months at nine. They want to know how to keep the baby small to avoid vaginal reconstructive surgery. They want to know how they can be Instagram bikini ready, sans filter, before their six-week postpartum appointment.

I am not one of these women. I did not ask you for any of these things. And I left your office more afraid than when I entered it.

What you said rocked me to my core. I don't remember how our appointment ended, but eventually I wound up where this essay began, in the lobby of a big Midtown hotel trying not to cry in public as I desperately attempted to check in.

I think about those three glass butterflies on the shelf in your office. Next to all your degrees.

You said they represented each one of your daughters.

I want to reach through time and space and gather all three of them into my arms and tell them that they are beautiful and perfectly imperfect and that no jean size or number on the scale will ever define their worth. I want to tell them they are loved and lovable no matter what. I want to tell them it will all be okay. I want to tell them all the things I try to tell myself in that moment as I sob out the pain of that encounter.

I rock myself as I cry and hold my knees to my chest and think of your daughters, those three butterflies, just hoping that their mother hasn't crushed their wings.

TOOTHPASTE

What's the proper term for them? A toothpaste squeezer? Holder? Decanter? I don't know. I should probably google it. But anyway, the apparatus that helps squeeze the toothpaste out of the tube so you get every last drop literally saved my marriage.

I guess "saved" is a strong word. That makes it seem like our marriage was in trouble. It wasn't. It was great. It was wonderful. It was thriving.

But you know how people say they have pet peeves when in actuality, they're harboring seething and almost unmanageable hatreds that cause them to act in ways they can't control? My husband's pet peeve is the way I squeeze the toothpaste tube.

Now I want to make something clear. I love my husband deeply. He is a kind, loving, sweet, fabulous man and an incredible partner. But this issue was almost the end of us.

Again, that's an exaggeration, but I'm a writer, okay? Sue me. Actually, please don't because that would be annoying and expensive for us both. Also, on what grounds are you suing me for here? All this goes to say, don't be mad if I embellish for the sake of storytelling. You're the one who bought this book.

Anyway, back on track.

I love order. I'm the one who bought a thousand stackable see-through containers for our pantry so I could make it look like a game of snack Tetris. I learned how to Marie Kondo our closet and now I won't let anyone fold the laundry but me because it has to be just so. I'm not a maniac; I just don't like chaos.

My husband enjoys order in a different way. Take, for example, the way we both eat hummus. I'm a messy eater. I'll go at a tub of hummus with no plan, just dipping chips in any which way. When I'm done it looks like our dog stuck her paws in there and swirled them around for a while. It's hummus, who cares?

I'll tell you who cares.

My husband cares.

He prefers clean lines. He uses the edge of the chip to create a nice even surface with each new nibble. Circular movements, symmetry. When he's done it looks just like it did when he first opened the container. He's a gentleman who knows how to properly eat a communal dip.

But I digress. That's just an example. He doesn't REALLY care all that much about the hummus. What we're here to talk about today is toothpaste. And how it almost ended my marriage. Again, hyperbole, but we've been over this already, so for storytelling's sake, it was almost the death of us.

I squeeze from the middle. I always have. I mean, why not, right? You just pick up the tube and you squeeze. The goal is to get the toothpaste on the toothbrush, right? (Just like the goal is to get the hummus ONTO my chip and INTO my mouth.) I don't give a shit about the toothpaste tube and how I've left it. But somebody else does.

At first it was fun. Every time he'd pick up the toothpaste tube, he'd laugh at me incredulously. And I'd just kind of shrug my shoulders.

Then the laughs subsided and it was no longer funny to him. It was annoying, and bewildering. How did I not understand? To him I was essentially ignoring the bottom real estate of the tube. I was making it harder, for both of us, by not squeezing from the bottom. It was inefficient. How could I not see that? He was confused, he was frustrated . . . And then? He just couldn't take it anymore.

Granted, I wasn't trying. I'm a sleepy person. I'm especially sleepy when I first wake up and when I am about to go to bed. I sleep like a fucking rock. And I'll go for eight hours, nine, ten. And still. SO. FUCKING. SLEEPY. All this to say, I'm really not thinking very clearly when brushing my teeth, much to my dentist's dismay. And I am really not thinking about the fucking tube of toothpaste.

Did he blame me for it? No. It's how I was made. Some of us come out good at math and adept at using a tube of toothpaste. Some of us come out with a bizarre ability to remember totally useless facts from fifteen years ago and a deep inability to squeeze a tube of toothpaste properly.

Needless to say, we were at a crossroads. Something had to be done. Our marriage was in PERILE. (Again not totally true, but also again . . . dramatic effect.)

Our friend had had one of these contraptions that we had admired while staying at his house a few weeks before. It was cool and understated, and looked chic sitting on the bathroom counter. We hunted around for cheaper ones, different ones, smaller ones, but inevitably, if we were going to take the plunge, this model felt like the right move. Eventually, after some deliberation, we ordered it.

And then, finally, it arrived.

The toothpaste squeezer-outer thingy. (Which, in case you were wondering, is the technical term.)

What a glorious invention! You just insert the tube of toothpaste, turn the knob, and it squeezes it out for you. You're unable to squeeze from the middle of the tube. It's foolproof, it's fuckup proof. It's efficient and effective, and it saved our marriage.

Sometimes at night when I'm brushing my teeth, I stare at it in wonder and think of the time before it came into our lives. I also get very mad that I didn't invent it myself and I imagine the fortune I didn't make and what I'd be doing with it if I had. But thanks to whoever DID invent it, our marital bathroom is now a happy one. No fighting, no saddened looks, no disappointment, and no oddly shaped toothpaste tube. Oh no. Those days are behind us. There are only good ones ahead. With an evenly dispensed tube of toothpaste and a happy marriage.

And tubs of uneven lumpy hummus. But that's a story for another day.

PUSSYCAT BOW

I want to beat all of you girls on that show."

My makeup artist's hand digs into the skin of my thigh, which she's been clutching for the last five minutes. We're in the greenroom at the *Today* show and Martha fucking Stewart is holding my book. I have a book. In and of itself, I'm having a hard time wrapping my mind around that, but I do, I have a book, and now Martha Stewart, who is currently wearing a denim shirt with a giant pussycat bow, is holding my book and looking at me like I'm gum stuck to the bottom of her shoe.

Just a little context if you haven't read it. My book is called *My First Popsicle*. It is an anthology of essays on food and feelings that I wrote and edited and somehow convinced a slew of brilliant humans to contribute to. Some of the essays have recipes that go along with them. Not all of them, but about half. I wouldn't exactly call it a cookbook, but it lives within the cookbook family. Let's say it's a second cousin by marriage. Anyway, back to the story . . .

A few seconds before Martha spat out her desire to beat me and my female castmates, her makeup artist had whisper-screamed in her ear, "*GIRLS! GIRLS!* SHE'S FROM *GIRLS!*" This was because she had waltzed into the greenroom with her posse, looked at me, and said, "You look familiar. Why do I know you? Should I know you? Are you an actress?"

Even now, I have a hard time describing her inflection. It was like

I was the person who had stolen the parking spot she'd been waiting twenty minutes for. I was the stewardess who told her she couldn't switch from her middle seat to one of the fully empty rows for "safety protocol reasons." I was the barista who told her we'd just run out of oat milk but would she prefer coconut? My sheer existence was annoying and frustrating and somehow an inconvenience to her.

THAT is how Martha Stewart said, "Should I know you?" to me in the greenroom of the *Today* show on the release date of my first book.

So, like I said, her makeup artist whisper-screamed, "*GIRLS! GIRLS!* SHE'S FROM *GIRLS*," and then Martha said, "I want to beat all of you girls on that show."

It wasn't cute, it wasn't facetious, she fucking MEANT it.

That's when my makeup artist dug her palm into my thigh and texted me (we'd been frantically texting each other throughout this entire interaction): "My vagina has literally inverted inside my body."

I told Martha that, yes, I was an actress, but that currently I was there promoting my book.

Her face remained in the same resting I'm-a-goddess-and-you're-a-gnat expression it had been in since she entered the room.

To clarify, I worship Martha Stewart. Has she fucked up? Sure. Who hasn't. But she's also a powerhouse who kept her head high and paid her dues and then went on with the show. I admire and respect her. I do think that she lies ever so slightly in her recipes about the temp or the cook time so that the result is always ever so slightly off when you try one, ensuring that nobody will ever be able to fully do it as well as she can. But look, that's a boss move, so again, I bow down. This is not a knock against the one and only Friesian-horse-owning, baking-wizard queen. It's just a fucking insane story of the first and only time I met her.

So, moving on.

After I said that yes, I was an actress, and, yes, I was on *Girls* (not addressing the fact that she wanted to dress us all down with a spatula), I told her that I was here promoting a book. The representative from my publisher who was there watching over things jumped in and thrust one of my books into Martha's deeply uninterested hands, at which point Martha started to flip through it as if it were something dirty that might infect her.

As this was happening, my entire glam team (hair, makeup, publicist) sneakily and stealthily started snapping pictures of Martha holding my book. And thank god they did and I have the proof of the encounter, because otherwise all I would have is this story to tell, which you might choose not to believe. Honestly, I might choose not to believe it too. But now, thanks to my lovely team, I have photographic evidence of this entire bizarre and glorious happenstance.

"Have you made all of the recipes in the book?" she asked.

No, "asked" is the wrong word. It was more like a dare. Or a nail-you-to-the-wall question a prosecutor would ask a defendant on the witness stand. It was a lose-lose. If I had made them, it felt like she'd assume I more than likely botched them. And if I hadn't, well . . .

I stared at the pussycat bow.

And then I went with the truth because I'm a truly horrible liar. I told her I hadn't made a single one. Hadn't so much as tried.

Her face said it all. It said "I knew it." It said "FRAUD." It said "Now I don't just want to beat you, I want to whip you into an egg white peak." Somehow, without even moving her mouth, she made it known that her eyes were rolling back into her head with boredom, all while holding my book in her hands like it was a used hot towel they give you on the airplane that she was ready to discard.

And then a PA from the *Today* show appeared.

"We're ready for you, Martha."

She tossed my book down on the table, and with that, she was gone to do her segment.

The rep from my publisher said it felt as if we'd all been called to the principal's office.

Martha Stewart had just semi-known who I was, been annoyed by my presence, told me she wanted to beat me, HELD MY BOOK in her hands (albeit reluctantly), and then disappeared in a puff of green smoke. Well, I mean, she left the greenroom.

And she did all of this while sporting a shirt with a GIANT. DENIM. PUSSYCAT BOW.

All of us left in the greenroom watched her segment live on mute, staring at that huge fucking bow and giggling about what had just happened. Pinching ourselves.

"One more time for the bow," my makeup artist texted me.

"DENIM," I responded.

Martha Stewart, thank you for being the highlight of my book tour. Thank you for that insane experience. Thank you for the best pâte brisée recipe I have ever found. And thank you, thank YOU, for wearing that denim pussycat bow top.

I will never forget any of it.

IT'S IN YOUR HEAD

I think you're just going to have to come to terms with the fact that you'll have to live the rest of your life in pain . . ."

I stared at the bizarre modern art sculpture behind his desk and then at the Santa Claus–looking man in a lab coat sitting in front of me. A doctor. THE BEST IN LOS ANGELES, according to one of the many plaques on his mosaic wall of accomplishments.

My eyes glazed over as he droned on about how living with chronic pain "isn't that bad," and trying to convince me that a lifetime of various painkillers could "get me through a day." An expert in his field had just told me that this was my life now?

At that moment, sitting in that man's office on an overly sunny LA afternoon, I had the first, last, and only suicidal thought I've ever had in my life. I thought about how high the building was and wondered if it was high enough to jump from with successful fatality. Did people even jump off buildings anymore? What if I hit someone upon landing? What if I hit a dog upon landing? I love dogs. I didn't want to kill a dog.

It was an incredibly long journey to figure out what was wrong with me. Much, much longer than it should have been. For six years I felt like I had the worst UTI of my life. I did not have a UTI; I didn't even have a yeast infection. Now, I never thought I would want a UTI. What woman in her right mind would WANT to feel like angry gnomes are living in her urethra? But I wanted one, badly. Because every time my tests came back negative, it meant I still didn't have an answer to what was causing my insane urinary frequency, unbearable pain during sex, and a vagina that felt like someone was trying to impregnate me with a Molotov cocktail.

Every test I took came back with a clean bill of health. And I took EVERY test. Urine, stool, blood, sonograms, X-rays, CT scans, MRIs— you name it, they did it to me. I was a living science experiment. Once they had exhausted every test known to man, once they had checked every box and still didn't know what was wrong with me, they just stopped caring. And then they told me I was crazy. Hysterical. No exaggeration, multiple doctors literally told me, "You are imagining this."

After enough men in white coats with fancy plaques tell you you're insane, you start to wonder . . . Am I insane? Because what other options are there? "The specialists with degrees must all be wrong" isn't a very strong argument.

So after seeing Dr. Number One Gyno in LA, I went to see Dr. Best Urologist on the West Side. He put me on six weeks of heavy-duty antibiotics for an STD I did not have. Antibiotics that he assured me had no side effects but which in reality made me heavily depressed and caused me to gain fifteen pounds of water weight. When I asked him if my puffy and depressive side effects were normal, he responded, "No, that wouldn't be from the drugs. The only thing the drugs could do is make you feel listless, out of sorts, exhausted, maybe melancholy. And there is the potential for water retention but it's unlikely." So, in other words, the definition of depression. And water weight. But when I pointed that out to him, he reassured me that the drugs weren't causing my side effects; that they must be from something else I was doing.

Next, Dr. Best Gyno on the East Side treated me for a vaginal infection he said I might have. Like something straight out of the Tower of London How-to-Torture book, he performed an incredibly antiquated treatment that I assume and sincerely hope has been outlawed for years: he poured chemical-grade acid into my vagina. Apparently it was supposed to burn away the infected tissue so that new healthy tissue could grow back. In reality all it did was cause more pain. I could barely walk because any form of friction would bring me to my knees in agony. He told me it would heal in a few weeks. Months later the pain had barely subsided. When I went to see him for a follow-up, he told me that my body must just be taking longer to heal than usual. Again, it was my fault. I waited longer, hoping that I would one day wake up pain-free, wanting this doctor to be right, wanting his treatment to work. But it didn't. When I went back to see him yet again, to tell him the procedure wasn't working and that I was still suffering, he said, "Perhaps the pain is emotional."

And then, of course, there's my favorite. He was older, definitely a grandfather type. His plaque boasted THE BEST UROLOGIST IN THE NATION. (I'm also pretty sure you can have one of those made on Etsy.) I told myself, His reputation is the best in the fucking nation, so he must be able to figure out what's wrong with me, right? His office was full of books and dimly lit, like a fancy library. When I walked in, he didn't even look up from his seat at his large mahogany desk.

"Sit down," he said.

I did.

"You're an actress, right?" he said.

I started to respond and he cut me off immediately.

"I know what's wrong with you," he said.

WELL, HALLELUJAH! Somebody knew how to fix me; this wise old man knew how to stop this crushing pain! I felt an overwhelming sense of relief.

He raised his eyes and glanced at me through his spectacles. And then he said, "I know your type. You're an uppity actress and you should learn to self-soothe, missy."

I was so stunned I almost couldn't respond. And all I could think to say was, "Do you want to examine me?" He shook his head and said, "I don't need to. This pain is in your head."

And there it was again. This time from the best in the nation: You're crazy.

I began to wonder if they were all right. Was I some kind of psycho? Sadist? Was I somehow creating or imagining this pain? Was I crazy?

I went on to see dozens more doctors, specialists, and psychiatrists— I even tried hypnosis—all with the same result: You're fine. It's in your head.

Until . . .

The first thing I noticed was her boots. She was wearing a pair of Balenciaga boots I had been coveting for ages. I immediately felt safe. This woman wore shoes I understood.

"I like your shoes," I said, and then I burst into racking sobs.

"Tell me what's wrong," she said.

And I did. I told her everything.

"I know exactly what's wrong with you," she said.

I braced myself for the prognosis of mental instability, which I had just come to expect at this point.

"Nine out of ten women who come into my office complain of the same exact symptoms and they all end up having the same thing. My dear, what you have is shockingly common. It's called pelvic floor dysfunction. One in three women have it and you can stop eating addicting pain pills like Tic Tacs because we can fix you with simple physical therapy."

I'm sorry . . . physical therapy? Physical therapy?!

I'd had my sex life, my work, and my sanity compromised. I'd taken more psychotropic drugs than an eighties child star, and had been insulted, demeaned, and reduced to a depressive, puffy shell of a human.

And my answer was in stretching?

I mean . . . great, but also . . . seriously?

As my vagina got better, I began to reflect. Before I met Dr. Balenciaga Boots, I was so far at my wit's end that I had truly started to believe that all these men with plaques were right, that maybe I was hysterical.

Yep. Female hysteria is still a very, very real medical diagnosis. (Are we still sending women to the woods to bleed during the full moon? Sadly . . . kind of.)

In retrospect, I wouldn't trade in my pain, because it taught me everything.

I learned the hard way that it is essential that we as women know our own bodies, that we trust them, and that we don't ever let someone tell us that what we are feeling isn't real. Because it IS—just the fact that you are feeling it makes it real.

"Hysterical" is a way to demean, to dismiss, to strip you of any sense of self or power in one word. To make you small and put you in your place. "Hysterical woman" is sister oppressor to "nasty woman"— it reduces you to a weak and unintelligent NOTHING.

Sadly, even beyond this experience I am no stranger to vaginal issues. Ever since I was a little girl I've had problems with my nether regions. Any woman reading this is probably nodding her head right now. In terms of our anatomy, it's like men were given an automatic car with the push-button start, and women were handed an original stick-shift Model T with an instruction manual in a made-up language, no gas in the tank, and faulty brakes. Our hardware is simply more complicated and, I'd venture to say, prone to drama?

I joke with one of my girlfriends that if you haven't had sex with your partner in a couple of weeks because you've been apart for whatever reason and then you have sex, your vagina acts like a grandma who's never seen porn before: she's scared, she's upset, she's a bit inflamed, she can't stop crying. You have to talk her off the ledge, remind her that she knows this, she's done this, many times. There's no need to freak out or develop a urinary tract infection. But pretty much without fail, she does.

A few years ago, I'd been shooting abroad for a number of months and had only been able to see my husband off and on, on stolen trips home or his trips out to me. There had been relations but not a ton. Then I got a few days off in a row. Our friends were hosting a trip to the Bahamas, so we jumped at the chance for a little romantic reconnection and met them there.

After a couple days of swimming nonstop in the ocean, sitting in wet bikini bottoms, and having more sex than I had in months, it didn't surprise me that at the end of day three I was starting to feel the classic twinge of discomfort between my legs.

It was around three o'clock on a Saturday. I was playing cornhole and losing, to nobody's surprise. (I once described basketball as "the one you play with your hands.") The longer I played, the harder I found it to ignore the faint "Danger, Will Robinson" vibes my urethra was sending me. I told myself, Don't freak, you're fine, it's just the good old gal being dramatic. After my pelvic floor experience, I now have protocol in place. I never travel without my meds, I know the stretches I need to do, and armed with the knowledge of what I have, the flares don't scare me as much anymore. But when I went up to change for dinner I found the burn between my legs harder to ignore, so I took some bladder-numbing pills and shoved a suppository up there for good measure.

On the ride to dinner, I realized that the drugs I'd taken about forty-five minutes earlier weren't taking effect; if anything, the discomfort had grown ever so slightly. An hour later, I was sitting at a table of joyous, talkative, drunken friends, clutching a napkin between my legs thinking, This is it, this is how I die. I went to the bathroom to pee, and when the stream of urine stopped, the pain that shot through my urethra made me gasp so loud that a woman outside the stall knocked and asked if I was okay as I sat on the toilet panting.

By the time we got back from dinner I was losing it. My sweet husband tried to talk me down.

"Tell me what it feels like," he said.

I described it, and to his credit, he said it sounded like a UTI. He knew the drill at this point. He told me it would be okay. Then eventually he fell asleep. And I crawled out to the couch to silently sob in the fetal position.

Eventually I called my gyno.

After describing my symptoms, she said, "This isn't normal. You need to go to the ER."

The ER?! But that's so inconvenient for everyone. People only go to the ER when serious things are happening.

To be completely honest, if my pain had been one decimal less, I don't think I would have gone. I would have tried to ride it out. But I knew I couldn't get on a plane like that; I knew I couldn't sit for one more second with the sensation I was experiencing. So we went to the ER. I clutched Evan's hand so hard in the cab on the way there that I think I broke the skin. And beyond the pain, the overriding thought I had was, What if all the tests come back normal? What if this is the beginning of another six years of unexplained pain? What if all the doctors tell you you're crazy again? I was terrified.

The doctor who treated me was sweet. He was gentle and soft-spoken. He examined me and said my uterus looked "upset." He had me pee in a cup and tested my urine.

While we waited for the results he suggested "honeymoon cystitis," which I mean, sure, but also abso-fucking-lutely not. I wanted to put his hand on my pelvis and transfer my pain to him. I needed him to understand the brain-reorganizing level that it was at. It felt like my nerves were melting from the inside out. That doesn't happen from some long-awaited sex.

After they gave me an IV of heavy-duty Tylenol (I was too afraid to take the morphine drip they offered—real missed opportunity) and my urine came back clear (which felt upsettingly familiar), the doctor said he wanted to do a CT scan of my abdomen. We ended up in radiology. Again a sweet doctor. He told me he had to inject me with a dye: "It's going to sting when it goes in and then make you feel like you have to pee, which is normal." It stung, but it couldn't touch the pain level I was already at. And then I sat in a cylindrical machine for the next thirty minutes trying not to wet myself and praying that the CT scan showed something, that this wouldn't be another case of phantom vaginal pain.

Turns out, it was an ovarian cyst that had burst. When the doctor came in and told me, the relief almost alleviated the pain I was in. I wasn't crazy, I hadn't made this up, something real and concrete and diagnosable had caused my pain. The CT scan had shown an abdomen filled with fluid floating around. I would find out weeks later at a checkup in Italy, where I had returned to shooting the TV show I was working on, that the liquid floating around inside me was blood. Sometimes cysts are filled with fluid and other times they are filled with blood. Blood apparently takes much longer to absorb, lucky me. The gynecologist who examined me was an older Italian man who spoke zero English. And because I speak zero Italian, a production assistant had to sit in on my exam in order to translate. Sadly, not the weirdest thing that's happened to me at work. Although this specific male Italian gyno did do something I'm not sure I'll ever get over. When he removed the speculum that had been inserted inside me, he put it up to his nose and smelled it like one would a cork on a wine bottle. If it weren't for the language barrier, I would have said something, but translating "What the literal fuck are you doing smelling my vaginal juices" felt like something I didn't want to put on that poor PA.

Apparently, bursting ovarian cysts are common. Somehow I made it to the age of thirty-five as a woman without knowing that every month we get cysts on our ovaries. And when we get our periods, they shed. BUT if they don't shed, or not all of them shed, then they grow, and eventually, because there isn't much real estate to speak of . . . THEY BURST. THEY FUCKING BURST. And they cause the kind of pain that makes you wish you were dead.

Here's the best part: there is no way to know if this is going to happen, there is no way to prevent it, and once it does happen, all you can do to deal with it is to hang on tight and pray the doctor is nice and wants to give you a morphine drip.

Thankfully, so far as they tell me, there are no long-lasting effects. Your body absorbs the unwanted liquid and you go on with your life as usual, with the addition of the trauma that ensued from the fireworks display in the vicinity of your sex organs.

So what's the moral of this fable, you ask? Why am I telling you all these tales about my front bottom?

Let me leave you with a short story to drive my point home. I shot a movie years ago with a male costar who was going through a particularly nasty divorce and was very angry at women. I was playing a "whore" and he my abusive pimp boyfriend. One night we were shooting a pretty violent sex scene where he was supposed to fuck me at gunpoint, and while we were rehearsing the scene he said, "Wouldn't it be so moving to fuck you with the gun? Wouldn't that just really up the stakes?" And all of the men around me nodded an enthusiastic yes.

So standing in front of the entire crew, director, and producers, I said yes. I told myself it was "for the sake of the movie." I told myself he wasn't actually going to fuck me with the gun; he would just make it look like he was. How bad could a "fake" gun angrily and aggressively being thrust up into my inner thigh—really be? I told myself it wasn't that big a deal.

But it was a big deal. It was awful and traumatic and unnecessary. And truthfully it was painful. And it left bruises all over my inner thighs and groin. But I let it happen because I didn't want to seem difficult. Because "difficult" for an actress, or really any woman, is an incurable leprosy that haunts you till the grave. It is the same mechanism within me that made me start to wonder if the doctors were right when they told me I was imagining my pain. It is the mechanism that makes us ignore our instincts or defer to someone else, that makes us not speak up or trust our own bodies. But never again. Never again to a doctor pouring acid inside me, or telling me I'm crazy, or overmedicating me just to get "the hysterical actress" out of their office. Never again to a costar sticking a firearm near my vagina "in the name of cinema" because they hate their soon-to-be ex-wife. Never again do we have to give anyone else power over our bodies. We are currently having that power stolen from us. The power to choose when we want a family, if we want a family, the freedom to care for our bodies how we see fit. So to every woman out there, I say hold on to that power, hold on for dear life. Because it is your fucking birthright.

And to every man out there who ever tried to strip me of MY power by telling me I was hysterical or imagining things or just too anxious, who essentially tried to lock me away in a room with yellow wallpaper, I say—politely, of course—go fuck yourself.

WIFEBEATER

Once upon a time I was invited to Paris Fashion Week, to a single show. It was an absolute whirlwind. I flew there, landed jet-lagged, went to a fitting, went back to my hotel to try to sleep, and couldn't, so I watched *Casino* on demand instead. I know that movie is long, but with the jet-lag haze it felt like it was eight hours. I ordered room service and I tried to sleep again.

A friend of mine who worked in the fashion industry was there as well, so we met up to go for a walk. I don't remember why, but we were discussing hot dogs. And the next day a paparazzi photo ran of the two of us walking and talking down Rue Saint-Honoré with the caption, "J'adore: Zosia Mamet and a friend discuss the merits of Paris Fashion Week while in the city." To this day we laugh about that. If they only knew that the true conversation was about meat links . . .

The trip is a blur. And I can't say that I particularly enjoyed it. That's not to say I don't want to ever go back, but it was too fast for me to form an opinion; my feet, and my internal clock, barely touched the ground.

It was the flight home, however, that made the whole thing worth it.

I shuffled onto my plane in my most acceptable sweats. I am not a believer in dressing up to be on an airplane. I am a believer in comfort. If I have to sit in a moisture-sucking tin can in the sky for a number of hours, I need to be wearing something that doesn't tug or cut in or add to my discomfort in any way, shape, or form. So I go sweat suits all the way.

As I was huddling into my window seat getting myself all situated for the nine hours of travel that awaited me, Anna Wintour walked onto the plane. It was like seeing a tiger walk into your local supermarket. Like, you know they exist, you just don't expect to see them in the wild in such close and mundane proximity. But there she was. Bob coiffed to perfection, sunglasses so big they acted as a face mask, and no luggage. Not so much as a handbag. She sat down, and I fell asleep.

I woke up a while later, I'm not sure what time or how long I'd been asleep. All I remember is I looked up and there was Anna Wintour emerging from the airplane bathroom in JEANS and A WIFE-BEATER. I pinched one hand with the other, wondering if I was perhaps seeing things, or maybe I was still asleep and this was a lucid dream of some sort, but no, I was very much awake. It was jarring, like watching the Queen do a keg stand or seeing a swan have diarrhea. She caught me looking at her and stared back at me with a look that said, Yes, that's right, what you're seeing is real. But if you tell, nobody will ever believe you. And then she took her seat, and I fell back asleep.

I woke up again as the captain came over the loudspeaker to say that we were making our initial descent into New York and everyone should get ready. I got up to pee one last time, and as I passed Anna Wintour's seat I saw that she had changed yet again. She was now in an entirely different outfit. A perfectly ironed dress, new jewelry, and new shoes, and her sunglasses armor had returned to her face. Where were these clothes coming from?! She was like Clark Kent or something. When we exited the plane she went first, and I was certain I'd see her grab a bag of SOME sort, explaining how she accomplished her quick changes, but there was nothing. She walked off as she'd come on, dressed impeccably without so much as a cell phone to weigh her down.

After I grabbed all of my shit and got off the plane, I looked in every direction and saw no sign of her. As if she'd simply vanished. To this day I wonder if I did in fact dream this, if it was merely a figment of my imagination, or a trick of the light. But then I think, No, I saw what I saw. And it's too good a story to think it wasn't real.

There's an urban myth that Bill Murray goes around to dive bars, sidles up to the bar, sits next to someone, grabs their drink, and takes a sip. Then he turns to them and says, "Nobody will believe you." I wonder if this is Anna's version of that. Fucking with the sweet, lowly, sweatsuit-wearing civilians just for the fun of it. Yes, you saw the empress of global fashion in a wifebeater on a commercial flight, but honey, it's your word against mine, and nobody's going to believe you.

Years after this event, I would have a very vivid sex dream about Miss Wintour. In it we are ferociously making out, and as I pull back to stare lovingly into her eyes, I think, Wow, this is so crazy and wild. How did we even get here? I never would have thought my life's path would have led me to falling in love with Anna Wintour, but here we are. How will I tell Evan? Does she have a partner? Will they be heartbroken? Wow, this is weird . . . And so on and so forth.

I woke up from that dream truly confused. I can say without a shadow of a doubt that I have never been attracted to Anna Wintour. And yes, I know that dreams are complex and nuanced and things are not always what they appear to be and Anna Wintour was probably not "Anna Wintour" in my dream or I was Anna Wintour or Anna Wintour was me.

But I have another theory. I think maybe Anna Wintour knows

that I saw her that day on the plane and she is incepting my dream just to fuck with me because she can.

We will never know the truth. And some things are better left a mystery. But I'm here to say that I'm pretty sure Anna Wintour and Kid Rock share a wardrobe item, and witnessing that has been a highlight along my life's journey.

BREAKFAST WITH DS

I'm hiding in the bathroom of the Four Seasons Hotel in LA having a full-blown panic attack. The thoughts playing on repeat are, Don't meet your heroes, and, What if he hates me?

About a year ago, I got one of those emails where you have to stare at your screen and keep rereading to make sure that you're not hallucinating and/or it wasn't sent to the wrong person.

My agent's assistant had emailed me to ask if she could give my address to David Sedaris, who had requested it because he wanted to write me a letter.

Cue me dropping dead.

I wrote back: I'm sorry WHAT?! DAVID FUCKING SEDARIS?!

I grew up in this industry, so famous people to me were always just people. They have marital issues, they pick their noses, they chew with their mouths open. They tell boring stories or aren't that funny in person. Or they are just as wonderful as the on-screen personas that made them so famous, but even then, at the end of the day, they're still just humans like the rest of us.

But authors? Authors are an entirely different ball game for me. Growing up as a lonely kid, books were my escape. Those who could turn words into sentences that cut through muscle and bone? Magicians! I worship authors.

David Sedaris has always been one of my top-five favorites.

I had done a piece for *The New York Times Magazine* a few weeks before to promote the show I was on. The premise had been a culture diary—what was I watching, listening to, reading, etc. And I had been reading David's latest book. I guess he always read the *NYT* mag and had seen that I'd talked about his book and wanted to write me a thank-you note. I crumbled into a glitter puddle. Honestly, if he'd never even written me, just his inquiry for my address would have been enough.

But he did. On a postcard that he'd collaged himself, he wrote me a note, which I promptly framed. I know this sounds creepy, but fans have done weirder things. David, if you're reading this, I don't know, don't think I'm weird, please.

We became pen pals of sorts. I figured life would most likely go downhill after that, because how much better could it get? And then I asked him to write an essay for my book *My First Popsicle*, and he said yes and I actually almost keeled over and dehydrated into a human Fruit Roll-Up.

But wait, there's more.

We'd started to email a bit once the book came into play because we needed to get into things like contracts. Well, we didn't, but our lawyers did and such. And a few months into the email correspondence he wrote me and asked if I was going to be in LA in the coming weeks because he and his husband, Hugh, were coming through and he wanted to know if I would like to have breakfast with them.

OH.

MY.

FUCKING.

GOD.

I mean. In the words of Jane Bennet, "Yes, a thousand times yes!!!!" But also FUUUUUUUCKKKKKKKKKKK.

Obviously I said yes because, well, duh. And then I proceeded to spin out like an astronaut outside Earth's orbit. I had a couple of weeks before our date, which gave me ample time to run the gamut of emotions and stress about every possible thing. What time should I get there? Obviously not late because that would be rude, so early for sure, but like what amount of early because too early would make me seem weird and desperate, but it couldn't be too close to on time because given LA traffic I might then actually run the risk of being late, which would be catastrophic.

And of course, what was I going to wear? I had to look nice but not too nice because I didn't want him to think I was trying too hard, but I didn't want to show up looking like the dirty troll I normally look like, but I couldn't look too bookish because he'd know that's what I was doing, but if I was too fashionable then he'd wonder if I was shallow.

And then the biggest question: What do I order?!

So obviously I made myself sick with worry in the weeks leading up to our breakfast date. When the day arrived, I obviously got there forty-five minutes too early because I was so terrified of being late. And I went into the bathroom to pee and then the nerves set in so intensely that I decided I could never leave the bathroom.

And then I did something I've never done before. I called my manager and told her she had to get me out of this meeting. I said she had to call David's agent and tell him I had come down with the stomach flu and couldn't make our breakfast. She asked me where I was and I told her I was hiding in the bathroom. She told me I had to go to the breakfast. I told her I had fused to the toilet I was sitting on and she had to call David's team and tell them I'd been abducted by aliens.

It went back and forth like this for a while. Me pleading with her every which way to Sunday to please figure out a way to get me out of it. Telling her I was too nervous, that I was certain I was going to act like an insane person and not be able to form words, and I couldn't do it. Her telling me I was being ridiculous, which I was, and that I had to buck up and get my ass out there. And that no, she couldn't tell David Sedaris's agent that I had run away to join a cult on a mountain without cell service so couldn't be reached.

So I hid in the bathroom until it seemed like I was reasonably early enough and I headed out to the hostess stand to tell her I was here to meet David Sedaris. She sat me at a table and he showed up five minutes later, exactly on time, with his husband, Hugh.

I was so beyond relieved Hugh was there to have another body present to absorb my pinball energy.

I ordered oatmeal, after silently spinning out about whether or not to get that or eggs because eggs would be messy and I would end up eating them with my hands, which would reveal to him the heathen that I am, but oatmeal might make him think that I'm boring or health conscious and therefore even more boring and predictably "actressy" and maybe he wouldn't want to be my friend. This internal tennis match happened as I listened to him talk about his travels to LA while nodding and smiling but also trying to deduce if I was nodding and smiling TOO much, making myself look like a deranged hyena . . . Let's just say the mental gymnastics before and at the top of this breakfast would have qualified me for the Olympic team.

The oatmeal was delicious, and we had an absolutely divine time. David was everything I thought he'd be and more. And Hugh was a goddamn delight. We talked about everything and nothing, and I made him laugh at one point, which basically is the best thing that's ever happened to me. It was all perfect and normal—we were just humans who like each other having a meal. I drove home on a fucking cloud of endorphins and caffeine having obviously obsessively consumed the coffee the waitress had continually refilled.

After, David wrote me an email saying what good manners I have, and I thought that was maybe the nicest thing anyone could ever say to me. I was so happy I didn't continue hiding in that bathroom (although I totally could have because the stalls were the size of some New York apartments), and the oatmeal was maybe the best I've ever had and I love oatmeal, so that's saying a lot.

And of course, I had breakfast with one of my heroes and he surpassed my expectations.

Given how well that went, I don't think I ever want to meet anyone else I admire for fear that they'd fall short. I do think the old adage "don't meet your heroes" more than often rings true. And since I got beyond lucky this time, I feel it best not to push it. I wouldn't want to be greedy—it's not good manners.

MY CHIN COULD BITE YOU

The hard part about an epiphany is what you do after you have one. A yoga teacher told me that once in the midst of an existential crisis. At the time, I wanted to punch her in the face because what the fuck am I supposed to do with that while in the eye of an emotional tailspin? But part of that desire to inflict harm upon her was because she was right.

I thought of her as this specific epiphany came upon me like the rising dawn. Okay, I have epiphanied—now what the hell do I do?

This particular epiphany had to do with the fact that I was no longer in my twenties, which I obviously knew. I am aware of my age and can, contrary to popular belief, keep track of the passage of time. But I suppose the deeper "aha" moment was that when I turned thirty I didn't just go from one decade to another; I didn't simply swap out a 3 for a 2. No, by leaving my twenties I had left Eden. The blissful, youthful exuberance of the decade between childhood and adulting was gone. Now I was vulnerable, afraid, and burdened with the knowledge of things like mortgage rates and colonoscopies.

This all came crashing down on me one evening when I was out to dinner with two girlfriends. I was thirty-one; they were both twenty-nine—a seemingly thin divide from a numbers standpoint. But by the time we left the restaurant, I came to feel as if we'd entered the metaverse and my trajectory of existence was on an entirely different plane than theirs. They were still naked, gleeful, and blissfully ignorant in Eden. I was jaded, tired, and working the night shift at a Taco Bell. Metaphorically speaking.

We'd all been friends for a few years. As actresses, we'd all worked together and were close in that way of people who live the same life, experience the same struggles, have to work for the same shithead producers—bonded by shared experience.

It was a lovely New York fall night. One of the girls and I had gone to see the other one in a play she was doing. And then we'd all gone out for drinks afterward. Three ladies on the town having a New York night, drinking wine and taking in culture and being supportive; girl power, intellectual activity, socializing, what an evening!

I was feeling not genuinely horrible about myself that night, which is a feat in and of itself. I was having a nice time. I sincerely like both these women and spending an evening with them talking about work and books and life felt good, it felt enriching.

And then I felt it. A dagger on my chin. One of those pesky little hairs that pop up seemingly out of thin air. How do those hairs grow that fast, and can they talk to my eyebrows and/or the hairs on my head, please? (Teach them your ways!)

I find the sheer sharpness of these hairs unsettling. If I were a superhero, these hairs could be part of my weapons arsenal. Cutting someone's eye out simply by thrusting my chin at them! Or maybe they're remnants from days gone by when the women used to have to stay home and tend the hearth. Maybe they were a kind of armor, like porcupine quills, meant to keep predators at bay. When they tried to maul our faces off, they would feel the hairs and fall back, run away, scared off by the razor-sharp density.

They're so vehemently stuck to you too, as if they really, really want to stay. There are times when I get a hold of one with my twee-

zers and I have to brace my elbow against the sink to get enough pur-
chase on it to yank it out of my face.

Anyway, you get the idea, or you know it yourself: these tiny chin
monsters are the worst. And as I sat there, chitchatting with these ladies over rosé, I felt one of them on my chin.

I audibly sighed.

The girls, concerned by my dismay, asked me what was wrong.

"Oh, it's nothing," I said, "just one of those fucking chin hairs."
Both of them stared at me like I had said something akin to Oh, it's
nothing, just one of those extra ears I grow on the back of my neck
from time to time.

"What chin hairs?" they asked.

This is when I knew—when the realization crystallized: I had
crossed over the line. I was now on the other side. I was other. I was
different. I was no longer in my twenties.

I couldn't help myself, and even though I knew it would just make
me feel worse, I tried to explain it to them. Maybe if I elaborated,
they'd suddenly realize what I was talking about and tell me they understood. That they got them too . . .

"You know," I said. "Those horrible little black jagged hairs that
pop up out of nowhere on your chin and feel like a tiny troll dagger is
popping out of your skin."

"No," they said. "We don't know about those. We have no idea
what you're talking about."

They weren't cruel about it. But they didn't try at all to hide their
confusion. Their not-knowingness. They stared at me with their
beautiful, bright, naive twentysomething eyeballs and I melted into
myself with despair. I was a troll. I was an ogre. I was a sea hag who
lived underneath a bridge and ate toads for breakfast and I was having
dinner with a wood nymph and a cloud sprite.

The evening ended nicely enough. I laughed it off and changed the subject to something mundane and we quickly found common ground again. But after we parted ways, I speed walked back to my apartment, fingering the hair as I walked, contorting my lips so I could feel the full length of it. Running through the front door and into the bathroom, I grabbed my tweezers and hunkered down in front of my magnifying mirror ready to go to battle with the tree trunk that had taken root in my skin. As I dug into my face, grabbing and pulling, grabbing and pulling, I thought of those two girls.

For now they slept on dewdrops and survived off honeysuckle breezes and dreams. They didn't know of ogre life. But someday they would find a hair on their chins at a fancy dinner and excuse themselves to the bathroom to try to rid themselves of the internal embarrassment of knowing they had a single five-o'clock shadow sprig.

I eventually got the hair. And I will say, when you pluck those bad boys, the satisfaction you feel almost makes the whole horrid experience fruitful. But I suppose that's true for anything disgusting or gruesome. The sheer fact of overcoming it, ridding yourself of it, almost makes the torment worth it.

Almost . . .

WANNA BE MY BEST FRIEND?

It's hard making friends as an adult.

And maybe I'm biased because I am a woman but I think it's MUCH harder making girlfriends as an adult. Girls are fucking weird, man. We're insecure and anxious and at times truly unhinged, and it's just hard to make a connection with another woman who is the same brand of insecure and anxious and unhinged.

When you meet at the sandbox at four or six or even ten, the self-awareness doesn't exist at that crippling level yet, so it's easier to let your freak flag fly and say something like, Hey, wanna be friends?

But once you hit your twenties, the self-consciousness suctions to you like a barnacle, and pretty much everything is done through the lens of "But what would people think of me if I did, said, wore, thought, was that?" The initial courtship phase is deeply fragile and intimate. It's like if you mixed modern dance with an Irish jig, staged it on melting ice, and did it in toe shoes made of glass.

When I first met Blanche, the initial thought that went through my head was, Oh my god she's so cool and nice and pretty and funny and smart, she obviously wouldn't want to be my friend. And then I thought, Don't fuck this up, Mamet. And then I thought, Sweet Jesus, please be my friend, I think I love you.

Look, I'm going to give you a spoiler alert because I know this is basically as much of a nail-biter as a Harlan Coben thriller, and I don't want you stressing out through this entire essay. It's been over a decade and Blanche is one of my best friends of all time. She's practically a sister to me. So you don't have to worry. But when I tell you about the disaster that was our first friendship date, you'll be agog at the fact that we made it this far, honestly that we made it at all. But hey, it just goes to show you, soulmates are meant to be together.

So here's the love story that is me and Blanche—Blanche and I? I'll never get that one right. Sorry, guys, I didn't go to college, but this is why we have editors, right? (Love you, Meg.) Back to the story.

I hate sports.

Okay, I don't HATE all sports. I love watching tennis and I enjoy watching sports from the comfort of my own home when there are stakes involved. If you asked me if I wanted to watch any old basketball game, I'd say, No, thanks, I'll be in the other room doing something else—literally anything else, like possibly plucking my eyelashes out one by one. But if you tell me it's the college seven or March Madness or whatever those playoff games are called where it's for the whole caboodle and there's an underdog story and the one team got here on unthinkable odds and it's the other team's coach's last year before retirement, I will be the one screaming at the screen and cheering and shushing people. I like stakes, I like a story. I've even been known to cry. If there's something on the line, I can become invested in an entire team in a matter of minutes and I can hate a team in a matter of seconds. My husband calls me a fair-weather fan.

Without the stakes I just don't care. So when I got invited to go to the Green Room (a fancy room at MetLife Stadium where there's food and drinks and massage chairs and famous people) to watch a regular old Jets game, I wasn't thrilled.

I should also add that I HATE football, even if there are stakes, because I will never be able to understand the rules. Everyone will say, "Oh, there's only fifteen minutes left in the game." Cut to three hours later, and somehow there's now fourteen and half minutes. How is that a thing? Or just when I think I finally understand what's going on, something will happen that is contrary to what I thought were the rules, so I'll say, "Hey guys, I thought that wasn't allowed," and they'll say, "Oh yeah, well it 'technically' isn't except for every other Wednesday in months that only have thirty days in them if it's under seventy degrees and one of the teams is wearing a primary color." So, I'm out on football.

My husband, on the other hand, loves sports and was brought up playing, watching, and rooting for all sports. Once, at a family function, when everyone was discussing what my sister-in-law's unborn child would choose as his main sport, I asked, "What if he doesn't want to play sports?" You would have thought I said, "What if he wants to wear diapers until he's sixteen?" That idea just was not an option.

So, all that to say, we were going to the Green Room at the Jets game.

We got to the stadium and I was already annoyed with the trip, the parking, the not being able to bring in a bag that isn't see-through. But a super nice guy greeted us to bring us up to the Green Room. And I will say it's nice. There's a gorgeous bar and a serious food spread and tables and seating outside so you can watch the game comfortably. Physically comfortably, that is—there's nothing to be done for the brain discomfort of attempting to understand how the rules of football work. The lovely guy shows us around and then he brings us to the bar and introduces us to his fiancée. "She hates football too. Maybe you guys will get along."

That was the first time I laid eyes on Blanche. She had long, gorgeous brown hair and a beautiful clean face without makeup, was wearing jeans and a leather jacket, and had the most beautiful smile. She beamed, like sunshine. I loved her instantly.

I don't really remember what we talked about that day. Probably mostly our hatred for sports. That first chat is always a little stilted and nervous. But we invited her and her fiancé over for dinner a few weeks later.

We were living in Brooklyn at the time and the subways you had to take to get to our house were an absolute nightmare. I would find out much later into our friendship that Blanche lives in fear of being late just as intensely as I do, and if she actually is late, the viable options are show up late or fake your own death and never speak to the person you're meeting ever again because the mortification isn't worth it. So apparently they were running late on their way to our house and Blanche wanted to turn around and ghost us for all eternity because she was so humiliated. Thank GOD her fiancé convinced her otherwise. I don't even remember them being late. I barely remember the dinner other than it was lovely.

What I do remember is that they had brought dessert. A vegan ice cream. Blanche went to serve it, and when she plunged the spoon into the ice cream carton and tried to extract a spoonful, it got stuck and a chunk of ice cream went flying into the air and lodged itself in her gorgeous brown locks. I just stared at her and knew that woman needed to be my best friend.

A few weeks later, Blanche and her fiancé invited us up to her family's cabin. It was about an hour-and-a-half drive out of the city. This was a big step on the friendship journey. Her fiancé was a golfer just like my husband. And Blanche loved to hike just like me. So the plan was that the boys would golf, Blanche and I would hike, we'd all go to the drive-in movie together that evening, and then dinner and a slumber party, and best friendship, here we come. What could possibly go wrong?

The cabin was really a bungalow, one that her parents had been renting in this gorgeous bungalow colony for eons. They were spending the day there too but leaving the bungalow to the kids for the overnight. So when we got there we were greeted by Blanche's family. Another big deal on the road to best friendship, meeting the parents. Just before we left, her mother shoved provisions at us, including a bag of cashews the size of a basketball (see my sports reference there?).

Blanche didn't drive. Having grown up in Manhattan, she didn't really have a reason to. So I drove the four of us to the golf course, where we dropped off the boys and then headed out to find a hike.

Picture this:

We drive to a nearby state park with a gorgeous hike up to a lookout with a view of the whole Hudson Valley. Sounds like a dream. But as we pull into the parking lot, a state trooper flags us down. He tells us that the mountain is "at capacity" and they aren't allowing anyone else into the park. How can a MOUNTAIN be at capacity? Like, does it have a weight limit? Is this an elevator? I was so mad at this state trooper throwing a major wrench in the plan of my first solo friend date with my (HOPEFULLY!) soon-to-be new best friend that I contemplated (1) attempting to sweet-talk my way into getting him to let us in, and/or (2) sounding off on him and debating the logic of a fucking mountain having a human limit. But I decided getting arrested on a first friend date wasn't the best look, so instead I thanked him and turned the car around.

Now, look, I will be the first one to tell you that Blanche is an angel. She works in the nonprofit sector, and she's a yoga teacher and an incredible mom of three (I honestly wish she'd adopt me—those kids won the mom lottery). She's a badass with a heart of gold. But nobody is perfect. And Blanche has one glaring flaw. She is mind-bendingly, earth-shatteringly, beyond-all-comprehension bad with directions. As one of the smartest humans I know, it defies all logic, but trust me when I say she couldn't find her way out of a paper bag.

We're in the middle of nowhere in upstate New York, surrounded by trees and deer and mountains that can't hold more than a certain number of people. I don't know this area at all. But Blanche says not to worry, she remembers there's another hike nearby that she loves. It's not quite as long or as strenuous as the one we were turned away from, but it'll still be beautiful. It's a gorgeous day, we're two new friends out for a first solo friend date, everything is groovy. I tell her that sounds great and I ask her how we get there. She says she isn't sure but she has a general idea.

Cue hapless driving for the next hour-plus.

Blanche's directions (if you can call them that) eventually land us at what seems to be more like a mound on a slight incline as opposed to a hike. We get out to explore this possibility but eventually get back in the car, because, well, to be honest, after walking up what was basically a short hill, we'd done what that "hike" had to offer.

We keep driving and she says she thinks there's another hike up ahead. I'm of course attempting to check my massive anxiety that this entire situation going tits up is my fault, and that Blanche hates me, thinks I am a loser, blames me for the mountain being at capacity, and is probably wishing she was anywhere else but in that car with me.

Eventually we come across the hike she was thinking about. There seem to be enough people to encourage us to explore further, so we grab our bags and set out with renewed energy, both determined to make this friendship date awesome if it's the last thing we do. We enter the trailhead and soon come to realize that this hike is basically just a loop around a lake. But at this point we've been in the car for most of this hang, so we decide to cut our losses and take this pretty stroll. Eventually we stop at a large rock and have a seat. Blanche pulls out a joint.

As someone with debilitating anxiety, I love weed. But at this time, I was just dipping my pinky toe back into the world of marijuana, terrified to have a repeat of the incident when I seventeen and accidentally smoked weed laced with crack and basically thought I was dying. My tolerance was still quite low. Blanche, on the other hand, was an expert, having been a bit of a partier in high school and college. When she pulled out this joint, I, of course, not wanting to seem like a square loser, was like, Yeah, totally whatevs, let's fully smoke this joint together! No big deal whatsoever, I'm cool!

So we start chitchatting away, passing the joint back and forth, our soon-to-be best friendship blossoming before our very eyes in this gorgeous wooded setting. Before I know it we've smoked the whole thing. Blanche suggests we keep walking and we set off again, strolling around the lake.

About fifteen seconds after we start walking, the weed hits me. It feels like my legs are melted Twizzlers and somebody has poured molasses all over my arms and turned up the ambient sound of the woods to eleven. My hands are fully numb, and my feet look like they are a thousand miles away from my face.

This is by far the most high I have been since my very own crackcident episode at the age of seventeen. I remember what that felt like, of course, so in this current moment I am aware enough to know that I am face-meltingly high. At the same time, I don't want to seem uncool or weird to this girl I'm falling so hard in friendship love with. So as we're walking, I take out my phone and attempt to muster enough hand-eye coordination to text my husband. I finally get a sentence typed out: "Got too high, freaking out," which I send, and then add: "Please don't tell her fiancé I don't want Blanche to think I'm uncool." Send. Only to be told seconds later that there is no cell service.

Blanche is walking in front of me and talking about something I can't understand. The energy it's taking to remember to breathe and put one foot in front of the other is almost painful. She turns around and asks if I'm all right. I try to give my best super-chill-yeah-everything-is-totally-cool laugh, which I think I pull off but in reality probably sounds like a squirrel being strangled.

We keep walking. It's a flat trail. My grandmother could have taken this walk. But we pass a family dressed in such extreme hiking gear I start to wonder if I'm so high that we're actually on some kind of Everest-esque hike and I don't even realize it. Do I think we're on a stroll but I'm actually scaling a mountain right now? This family is dressed in long pants, long sleeves, full wide-brimmed hats. They have massive backpacks spilling over with climbing ropes and carabiners and are walking with very professional-looking walking sticks. I chalk it up to the weed and convince myself I'm seeing things.

Until a couple of minutes later, when we see what looks to be the same exact family walking past us in the same direction decked out in the same hard-core hiking gear and I start to truly lose it. I try breathing through my nose, I try shaking my hands, I try anything that I think will calm me down and make me look normal. I convince myself that Blanche can't tell that I'm having a full-system meltdown. Right?

We eventually make it all the way around the lake and back to the parking lot. Blanche suggests we get in the car and make our way back to the golf course, where we're meant to be picking up the boys. Still attempting to act cool and breezy, I agree and I get in the car. I go to punch in the directions for the golf course, only to be told again by my phone that there is no service. I turn to Blanche and ask her if she knows how to get back to the golf course and she looks at me like I had just asked her if she could recite pi from memory. And then I remember that she can't drive either.

That's when I lose it.

The words come out of me like liquid diarrhea after bad Mexican food. I tell her that I have barely smoked pot since my bad experience when I was seventeen. That since then I've only done it with my husband in the comfort of our home and in my pajamas. I tell her that I'm convinced we just scaled a mountain and I don't know how we survived. I tell her that I don't think I can drive and I don't know when I'll be able to and I know she can't drive and my phone doesn't work so I can't reach the boys.

And then I take it up a notch because everyone knows once you let a spiral get going it's hard to pull back. I tell her that I realize we're stranded and I wonder if we have enough food to ration because who knows how long we're going to be there. The boys don't know where we are, they thought we were going to the mountain we were turned away from, and with no service, we have no way of telling them our location. And without service my GPS doesn't work and Blanche can't direct us and I don't know the area so I'm no help in that department either so we basically are lost in the woods. I tell her I don't have any heavier layers or blankets in the car and I don't know how cold it gets up there at night in July and if we run out of gas in the car we won't be able to turn on the heat and I'm afraid we might freeze to death. I tell her I don't think we can drink the lake water and we only have what's left in our water bottles and I didn't see a drinking fountain so if we don't freeze to death we might die of dehydration. I tell her I'm sorry and I hope someday she can forgive me, that is if we get out of this alive.

She suggests we get out of the car and go sit in the sunshine. So we do. There are kids playing and I remember watching them and thinking about how fleeting life is. How innocent they looked. How safe they must have felt in that moment. Blanche takes out the industrial-sized bag of cashews her mother had handed to us before we left, which now felt like years ago.

"Have some cashews," she says. "It might make you feel better."

But even though I'm as high as a lost balloon, I'm not hungry. So we both sit there looking like two crazies in the middle of the parking lot, chilling on the ground, as she munches away on the cashews that I refuse to eat.

Every few minutes, she says, "Have some cashews. It might make you feel better."

But every time she offers me handful I shake my head.

She just keeps offering. Like these cashews are the solution to all of our problems. Like these are magic cashews that have the ability to bring me down to earth, to make me capable of driving, to end my weed-induced panic spiral and make me feel my hands again.

As I sit there I, of course, start to catastrophize. I think about how sad it is that I ruined what I thought could have been a beautiful friendship. I think about all the things Blanche will tell her fiancé. How they'll laugh about me and what an insane loser I am.

Blanche continues to try to force-feed me cashews. I continue to refuse. What feels like seven years go by. And finally I think I might be able to drive.

On the drive back to the golf course, I am terrified to the point of nausea that I am driving like an insane person and that I am going to get pulled over and go to jail for the rest of my adult life. But somehow by the grace of all things holy, we make it to the golf course (how we figured out the way there nobody will ever know), where my husband tells me he had indeed gotten my text messages but the "Don't tell her fiancé" one had come in about fifteen minutes after the first, and he had indeed told her fiancé.

So now everyone knew that I had smoked too much weed, had a major panic attack, and (in my head) ruined the entire weekend.

The rest of the night is a blur. I remember we went to the drive-in movie but I couldn't tell you for the life of me what it was that we saw. I do remember sitting there watching and continuing to feel so sad at the potential friendship I'd ruined.

It's funny, the stories we tell ourselves—the realities we can create out of minuscule kernels, the yarns we weave. The brain is a powerful thing and anxiety will create a wildfire if you give it so much as an ember. I didn't ruin the friendship. The next morning, as we were leaving, Blanche asked if I wanted to go to a yoga class with her that week. I figured it was a pity invite, but in truth, it was simply the beginning of our friendship.

After over a decade of friendship, Blanche and I still laugh about this first date of ours. We've had so many experiences since that were better, worse, and way more mortifying than this ever was. But that's what best friends are for, right? To this day, whenever we're around cashews we can't help but laugh. I'm still convinced we entered some kind of space-time continuum on that walk around the lake and I don't think it was the pot. But I guess we'll never know.

Oh, and the only bad thing about our friendship? Our husbands will never let us forget that it wouldn't exist without football.

SHOSH

I miss her. I think about her all the time. I wonder what she's doing, who she's talking to, if her marriage survived. I often want to call her and ask. Text her and request updates, a coffee date, a drink to catch up. But I can't. Because she isn't real.

Except, somehow . . . she is.

I don't really have a process as an actor. I didn't go to school, I never had proper training. I do not write my character's backstory or try to remember when my cat died for emotional scenes or go method and not sleep when I'm meant to be sleep deprived. I learn my lines backwards and forwards so I can literally recite them without thinking, I show up on time, I make sure (to the best of my ability) that I am prepared in all the ways I can be: well fed, well rested, ready to go. And then I dive in. My husband likes to say I "shoot from the hip" and I think he's right. I am not saying this is right or wrong, but for me, this is how I do it: I find it in the moment on the day while the cameras are rolling. It is how I have always been. It is the part of my job that I love the most, because it feels like a free fall, a blackout, a total release for the moment that I am in the scene. And then the director calls "Cut" and I come back down to earth.

This isn't to say that the characters I play don't feel three-dimensional to me; they do, absolutely. But I don't take them with me. I don't embody them beyond the parameters of the moments that they are living and breathing within the scene.

Except for her. She was the exception to the rule.

Shoshanna, Shosh, Shoshers.

My mother once told me a story about falling through the ice when she was skating as a child on a pond that hadn't properly frozen over. She said when she took her jeans off they stood up on their own because they were so completely frozen through. And that is how Shoshanna feels to me—like a pair of frozen jeans, a material that should not but in this rare instance does stand up completely on its own. I like to joke that she came to being like Aphrodite, emerging fully formed from a seashell out of the ocean.

When I made my audition tape I did not prep beyond learning my lines. I ran those four pages of my audition scene over and over and over again until I could say them upside down and sideways and probably backwards if put to the test. And then when I went to record my audition tape, I did a single take of the scene. Sometimes when I'm really in the moment it feels similar to how I've heard people describe rage blackouts. You remember the moment before and the moment you come to, but everything in the middle is a black void of nothingness. And that's how it felt, like I, Zosia, went offline to make space for Shosh to take over for that period of time. She came out of me as if she had been a part of me forever, lying dormant just waiting for her time to arrive and come alive. Like a ghost possessing my body. I just had to open myself up to her and she was right there.

It started when we were shooting. I would have moments on my days off or over the weekend when I would get the urge to text her and ask what she was up to, how her weekend was going, what she was doing that evening. Which would of course immediately be followed by the forehead slap because you cannot text a fictional character, she does not have a phone or a data plan or opposable thumbs because she isn't real. But the urges would come all the same. I often get the same ones in reference to my dog, wanting to text Moose and let her know I'll be home in thirty minutes and ask if she needs anything from the grocery store only to remember that she is a dog, also sans thumbs, and won't be able to text me back.

Playing Shosh was one of the greatest joys of my life. Especially when they'd let me improvise. They would keep the cameras rolling and just let me go and words would tumble out of me like a frantic, girly, Technicolor dusty-rose yawn. There was a scene that we shot during our first season where I'm meant to be doing yoga in my apartment and I'm saging my bedroom in preparation. There were some scripted lines, but then, like they always did, on our last take they told me to just go for it, to improv whatever I wanted, and so I did. I think they let me go for a solid five minutes but it felt like five hours, it just kept coming out of me. Shoshanna setting intentions and wishes as she saged her bedroom walking back and forth over a yoga mat. I could have kept going; she could have kept going.

There are more of these moments when I was allowed to just entirely live as Shoshanna. There is a shot during the crackcident episode where she is running down the street in Bushwick high on crack. The camera was mounted on the back of a car that was tracking in front of me as I ran. And as we did it again and again, our director, Jesse Peretz, just told me to sound off, and so I did. And in that moment yet again I was not Zosia Mamet acting, I was Shoshanna Shapiro, high as a kite on crack cocaine for the first and only time spouting absolute nonsense about absolutely nothing from my crack-addled brain while running through the streets of Brooklyn in the middle of the night. I was her, she was me, and we were one.

Every time I'd read a scene, whether it be funny or sad and heartwarming, I'd have emotions about it in reference to her. I always feel for the characters I'm playing, I am empathetic toward them, I imagine every actor is, but normally I do not feel things as the character when I'm simply reading their lines on the page. My characters are usually separate from me, third-party entities that exist in a play world.

Except for Shosh. She was both a part of me and a person outside of me that existed on her own who I loved and was in relationship to and with. When she broke up with Ray I wanted to show up at her apartment with wine and takeout and hugs. When she lost her virginity I wanted to take her out to celebrate. When she sounded off at the beach house I wanted to call her and tell her I was proud of her. I wanted to visit her in Japan. I wanted to congratulate her on her engagement. Every experience she had felt wholly and utterly real to me.

She is the most intrinsically different from me of any character I have ever played. She is girly where I am a tomboy, owning ten different kinds of hair products to my not even knowing how to use a blow-dryer. She is positive where I am jaded, always looking on the bright side where I lean more toward the let's-catastrophize-this camp. She loves a tight fit and a cinched waist and a high heel, whereas I prioritize comfort over all, always looking for the closest thing to baggy pajamas that I can get away with in the real world that will look cute with sneakers. In every outfit I wore of hers, I felt like I was suffocating and about to break an ankle. Every outfit of mine she would probably look at with disgust and an audible "Ew." She is a speed-talking Energizer Bunny who loves pink and is more than likely running a Fortune 500 company and on her second marriage to a highly successful hedge fund manager. I need nine hours of sleep to be fully functional, my favorite color (if I'm being honest and not saying navy) is black, I barely graduated high school because I couldn't pass algebra, and I married another actor.

I've often said the trickiest scenario I run into with fans is when girls come up to me expecting to meet Shosh and instead they get Zosia. I am the foul-mouthed, tattoo-covered, teenage-skater-boy, spicy-margarita counterpart to her pink-velour-wearing, champagne-with-strawberries, bubbly sorority-girl-ness. We could not be more different if we tried. When girls used to come up to me thinking that I am her and wanting to connect and commiserate because they too felt like and were experiencing all that she was, instead they would get me, greeting them with a "Hey, man" and most likely dirty hair, my voice five decibels lower and twenty-five RPMs slower.

It killed me to see the wash of disappointment over their faces when they realized I wasn't her. I always wanted to apologize and suggest we get her on the line so she could make us both feel better. But sadly I do not yet have that power. I tried to at least share in their love for her, which sometimes made the situation moderately better. But overall these encounters always served as a reminder of how truly other than me she is, and yet how whole she feels to me.

I am a fast talker. But NOTHING on her level. I'm not even sure where that decision came from—that's just what came out of me when I said those lines. We have something called additional dialogue recording (ADR) that we have to do as actors. It's when there is an issue with the dialogue from a scene, like it was too windy so we sound muffled or the other actor stepped on your line and yours isn't super clear or perhaps there were dogs barking or sirens or a baby crying—anything that makes the current dialogue unusable. When this happens we have to go into a sound booth and rerecord audio to match what we are doing on camera. The sound engineers then lay in the new dialogue over the old dialogue and voilà, movie magic!

ADR is not easy; re-creating a performance or even just matching the dialogue is tricky, but for Shosh it was damn near impossible.

Every time I had to do ADR I was totally in awe of how fast I was talking and nearly unable to match her speed. Just another example of how she possessed and entirely took over my body. I, Zosia, cannot talk even close to how fast she can. That girl has a speedboat for a mouth.

Before every table read and at the beginning of every new episode, I would have a bit of a mini panic attack, worried that I wouldn't be able to find her again, that she wouldn't show up. But then we would read the scene or the director would call "Action" and there she would be waiting, like she always was.

There is a poem, I cannot remember who by, about a girl who is working on a farm out in the fields when she senses a storm of inspiration coming. She races back to her house trying to beat the storm because she knows if she doesn't catch it, it will pass. She makes it home just as it is approaching overhead and she catches her pencil just in time for the lightning of creativity to strike and the poem rushes out of her through her pencil onto the page.

I often think this is what Shoshanna was for me. She was a lightning strike, a deep thundercrack that I was lucky enough to capture and harness. I happened to be in just the right place at the right time for her to move through me. Perhaps she is a ghost from another time. Maybe she is even a relative of mine that I inadvertently called to the present. I will never totally know nor do I ever truly want to understand the magic of her because somehow it feels like putting her under the microscope and investigating would diminish her power, which I never want to do. Instead I am content to just feel eternally grateful and fortunate that I got to commune with her for that period of time. That she picked me. That Lena Dunham and Jenni Konner and Sarah Heyward and all our other brilliant writers helped create her three-dimensional existence and allowed me to be the one to play her.

I do not think I will ever stop missing her or wondering what she's up to or wishing I could call her and catch up. But wherever she is, whatever she is doing, I know that she is killing it, that she is looking fabulous while doing it, and that she is always and forever having the last laugh.

Epilogue

THEN THEY WENT AWAY

When I was a little girl I had a whole catalog of songs that I made up and would sing on regular rotation. My family lovingly refers to them as "Zosia's Greatest Hits." When I think on them now, I wonder what was swirling around in my tiny brain, because the songs are strange.

Strange beyond the realm of normal childhood weirdness.

The oddest one is probably "Nineteen Little Bunnies," a ditty about nineteen bunnies hopping through a mirror. What that meant to my four-year-old brain we will never know. But the thing that strikes me the most is the line that's featured in this song, and which appears in many of my other greatest hits: "Then they went away." (Or, as it sounded in my toddler dialect, "Den den went away.")

Even as a small child, the thing I thought of most, the thing I infused my creative musing with, was the thought of everyone. Always. Leaving.

-‹‹‹◆›››-

When I was growing up, my therapist used to tell me I had a hole in my piggy bank. That any time someone showed me love or I accomplished a goal in my recovery, had a career success, or made a friend, I would put that token into my piggy bank and it would fall out of the hole in the bottom. So every time I shook my piggy bank it sounded hollow, empty, broke. I lived my life with the perception that I'd done nothing, accomplished nothing, that nobody loved me, blind to the huge pile of coins laying on the floor underneath my porcelain pig.

I get it from my family.

I come from a line of people whose default method of existing is living with a constant undercurrent of fear: fear the money will disappear, fear of illness descending, fear of the world slowly melting toward its inevitable end. We're not alone in those fears. But the biggest and most pervasive fear within my family is that of not being enough—not having done enough and therefore not being lovable, and that if we're not lovable enough, eventually everyone around us will leave.

Yes, my family is full of doers and achievers who have accomplished great success. But that success was not a relief to any of them. It did not make them feel safe or secure. In fact, it did the exact opposite. Because once the job is gotten or the good reviews have come in, you are exposed again. It feels like you are sent back to square one. Things do not last but rather have to be re-earned every day, starting from scratch. Someone's love, someone's respect, someone's adoration, or the building blocks of a career. In my family these are not things you bank and build upon but things you lose every time the slate is washed clean. It is a terrifying feeling. It is overwhelming and daunting and it makes the need for these things—love, approval, fame, money—feel almost primal.

The fear wasn't something my parents actively passed down on purpose. They didn't sit me down at the dinner table and draw me a diagram explaining the statistics of this inescapable outcome. Rather, they taught me through their actions. And, as we all know, children learn by example.

This is what I learned from them: you are never enough.

-«‹‹◆››»-

When I was growing up, my mother was always buying new Armani suits. I would sit on the floor of her closet as she would try them on, telling me how expensive they were, how she really couldn't afford them, but that they were a necessary cost to doing business—she had to have the nicest suits for her auditions, the most expensive, the most perfectly tailored. I think to her they were a sort of armor. She thought if she walked in wearing the perfect suit, somehow it could protect her from rejection.

She also made me run lines with her for auditions, and if she flubbed one or couldn't remember one, she would bitch about how terribly it was written, how people didn't talk that way, how unnatural the wording was. If the words were bad, maybe it was okay if she didn't get the part, because who wanted it anyway.

It probably didn't help that on every opening night of one of my mother's plays, my grandmother would come backstage, and before offering congratulations or even so much as a hug, the first words out of her mouth would be notes—on the play, on my mother's performance, on all the ways in which it could have been tighter, stronger, better.

Eventually my mother stopped auditioning entirely. She blames circumstances and the industry and the fact that nobody writes for women her age, but I suspect it is because she feels safer removing herself from the line of fire. She would rather not even try for success than risk the potential rejection on the journey to get it.

My father isn't much different.

The only movies or TV shows made after the year 1985 that he considers any good are those that are so completely different from anything he ever could have made himself.

Or foreign-language films.

Once, when my stepmother was on vacation with my half siblings in Scotland, my father and I got tickets to see *Inglourious Basterds* on opening weekend. We went to the Grove and saw it on one of the biggest screens they had. The theater was packed to the brim, and we sat center row, center aisle—smack-dab in the middle of the theater. My father is hard of hearing and thinks because he is, everyone else is too. So ten minutes into the film he turned to me and, in what he thought was a whisper, yelled, "This is a piece of shit, we're leaving." And then he got up and made his way out of the theater, blocking the screen for half of the humans trying to watch. The whole time he was muttering, loudly, what absolute trash we were watching and what a hack Tarantino is.

Or take the time I found him sitting in his reading chair, which is to the left of the fireplace and nestled underneath a set of bookshelves built into the wall. I had come home from school and found him there staring into space. He was in his pajamas, holding an empty cup of tea, and just staring at nothing. He looked inconsolably sad. Like a man with the entire weight of the world crushing down on him. In fact, he was so focused, he didn't see me when I walked in. I cleared my throat to get his attention and asked him if he was all right. He slowly looked up at me and asked with complete sincerity, "Do you think I've accomplished anything with my life?" I looked to the bookshelf behind him, to the shelf directly above his head where, like a halo, sits his Pulitzer Prize.

-《《◆》》-

I say all of this not to dump on my family or to label them as ridiculous or extreme.

None of these insecurities are unique. Hollywood is a brutal industry and these feelings run amok. You would be hard-pressed to find a creative person who isn't threatened by their contemporaries' successes or doesn't fear rejection.

No, I'm telling you all of this as an explanation, for me, for why I am the way I am, why I sang as a child about everyone leaving, for why I gave the book this title, for why I wrote it in the first place. Because of course, given what I was taught and how I was made, I am terrified that everyone reading this now hates me, thinks I am a hack, a terrible writer, a narcissist, a loser with unfunny stories who is delusional in thinking that anyone would want to read about my life.

I have worked incredibly hard to quiet this Gollum-like voice in my brain. But the truth of the matter is that pretty much everything I do in this life is finished with a question mark. Does this make me funny? Was that take good enough? Am I a good wife, partner, dog/horse mother, friend? Was that the right response to someone telling me their parent is ill? Was that too big a meal? Too small a meal? Did I work out enough this week? Did I work out too much? Should I write this book? Should I fake my death and anonymously return my advance and change my identity and move to a small island in the Philippines so I don't have to publish this book and deal with the opinions everyone will have about it?

The question mark is the punctuation to the fear of myself. I do not trust myself or my ability or my talent or my instincts. Because I was taught not to. Because nobody in my family does. Because when you have a void to fill you can't trust yourself. Every day is spent in pursuit of the thing that will fill that void and so the overarching feeling you live your life with is fear, fear that today you will not fill that void and that tomorrow the hole will be even bigger.

-‹‹‹◆›››-

My husband and I recently had dinner with some friends and the topic of fame surfaced. One of our friends posed an interesting question to everyone at the table: "If there was a button that you could press right now and immediately have more fame, would you press it?"

The answers were fascinating and, for the most part, unanimous. Everyone said that even though more fame seemed appealing, inevitably the way it would alter your life and the sacrifices you'd have to make in exchange for the fame didn't seem worth it. Even though money can give you the chance to do more good, and you can ensure an ease of living for yourself and your loved ones, we all agreed that more money isn't necessarily a guarantee.

So everyone answered no.

And then it was my turn.

I understand how cringe it is to desire fame. I also understand that if you are reading this book, you are probably thinking, Objectively, she is famous, she is successful, she has gotten the thing she so badly wanted. I get all of this. I understand that the cool answer to this debate would have been, No, of course I'm not pushing the button. I don't need it, I don't want it, I am whole without it. But that would have been a lie.

These were good friends, close friends, and when it was my turn I thought about lying, but (a) I knew they'd all be able to tell if I was hedging, and (b) I didn't want to lie. So I answered truthfully. I told them all that absolutely without question I would press the button. That even though I know all the sacrifices that come with fame, and that it is not a magic bullet and that historically speaking we have seen time and time again that the most famous people end up being the most deeply lonely and miserable, I still want it.

Because of that hole in my piggy bank. It is part of who I am.

I have been taught and now believe that the love and adoration and approval of others is the only thing that will make me whole. Just in the same way that I thought being skinny would make me lovable, I think fame will too.

To me, these things are the ultimate safeguards. If I am skinny, I am safe, because nobody will leave if I am skinny. If I am famous, I am safe, because nobody can tell me I am not enough if I am famous. It is whole-body armor; it is a fairy tale I tell myself.

I've tried to let it go. And I have been somewhat successful. There has been growth, vines that have begun to knit over the void. I no longer starve myself in an attempt to be lovable. I no longer think (entirely) I am only as good as my last job. I no longer have full-fledged panic attacks after every audition because the thought of not getting the job makes me wonder if I even deserve to be on this planet.

And yet I would still push the button. Because even the possibility of becoming famous enough to fill the void is too alluring to say no to. I know that isn't real, I know fame will not keep them from leaving, and yet . . .

―≪≪◆≫≫―

When I first started to gain some success my father told me not to read reviews. When I asked him why, he said, "Because the good ones are never good enough. And the bad ones are all that you'll remember."

So I'm going to do my best not to read reviews for this book.

I'm going to sit on my metaphorical floor and attempt to duct-tape the hole in my piggy bank.

I'm going to try not to ask you, Does this make me funny?

I'm going to try not to care what your answer is—if it's yes, if it's no, if it's maybe. I'm going to remind myself it doesn't really matter.

Because if you made it this far, it means you didn't leave.

xx

ZM

Acknowledgments

I never planned on writing this book. The idea of writing a book about my life had not been on my agenda until Meg Leder came into my life. I was pitching *My First Popsicle* to publishers and during our meeting she asked if I had ever considered writing a book of personal essays. She referenced my essays I'd written for *Glamour* magazine and explained she basically saw it as a built-out collection of those. I had loved writing those essays, so I said yes. We still had to make *Popsicle*; that would take ages. And if I'm being honest, I think there was a very large part of me that figured that when it came time for me to write this book everyone would have forgotten about it. That was not the case . . . This book has been a journey for me. I have now come to learn from speaking to other writers that for the most part writing is not something they find enjoyable. The act of HAVING written is, but the actual process is torture. I stand here today with the same sentiment.

That being said, I am grateful that I was encouraged to write this book and that would not have happened without Meg. I could not have asked for a better editor if I had written her myself. Meg, you are everything I needed and then some. Firm when I needed boundaries, and yet you gave me grace and time to explore. You were ever encouraging but laser focused with your edits. And from day one you understood who I was as a writer and storyteller and did everything in your power to foster that. I am forever grateful to you as an editor and as a friend.

To my unofficial editor, Sally Ware, the same sentiment applies. Every sentence I wrote, Sally was the first to read. She was the gatekeeper of the words that ended up in this book. Thank you for never lying or sugarcoating your thoughts and feelings on my writing. Because you shot straight about every word I sent you, I knew I could trust it when something passed your test. Thank you for reading and rereading and giving notes at all hours of the day and all days of the week. Thank you for always being there. I could not do any of this without you.

And thank you so much to Isabelle Alexander for coming in as a second pair of eyes and for taking over as my editor while Meg was on sabbatical. I so appreciate you jumping in as part of this team. Your help was invaluable and so deeply appreciated.

Thank you to my book agent, Melissa Flashman, for believing from the beginning that I could be a writer. Thank you for being patient, Mel, and never pushing me but always having faith.

Thank you to my husband, Evan, for being my sounding board and just generally being my rock in all the ways. For loving me exactly as I am, neuroses, weirdness, anxieties, and all, and for putting up with me making the most bizarre noises while expressing my frustration while editing this book.

And lastly, thank you to all the humans who have come into and out of my life to create all the experiences that gave me these stories to tell. Good, bad, ugly, and otherwise, you have all shaped my life. Some of you have permanent places in my heart. Some of you have permanent places on my shit list. But all of you have contributed to the fabric of my being. All of you had a hand in making me a storyteller. So, I suppose, all of you also had a hand in making me a writer. And for that, I thank you.